New approaches to manpower planning and analysis

New approaches to manpower planning and analysis

Edited by
P. Richards and R. Amjad

INTERNATIONAL LABOUR OFFICE   GENEVA

Richards, P.; Amjad, R. (eds.)
New approaches to manpower planning and analysis
Geneva, International Labour Office, 1994

/Conference report/, /Manpower planning/, /Manpower needs/, /Labour market/, /Developing country/. 13.01.2
ISBN 92-2-109183-X

HF
5549.5
. M3
N39
1994

ILO Cataloguing in Publication Data

Preface

Over the past decades, manpower planning was considered to be one of the means to create conditions for growth and sustainable development through an efficient use of human resources. Governments in many developing countries have received advice and assistance from the ILO in their efforts to improve their policies and techniques of manpower planning and, to integrate them better with overall economic, social and labour market policies. By the beginning of the 1990s, however, both the concept and effectiveness of manpower planning were increasingly challenged. This was linked, first, to the increased adherence to markets as the means to bring labour demand and supply into balance and, second, to growing evidence of the limitations of manpower planning in forecasting manpower needs accurately. In the euphoria of market liberalization and decentralized decision-making, some critics saw manpower planning as a concept related to the centralized planning of the past and emphasized its limitations rather than its potentialities in bringing about more and better employment through government action.

It was within this context that the ILO organized a workshop on new approaches to manpower planning and analysis in October 1991. The participants included a number of experts who had assisted governments, especially in the developing countries, in the development and implementation of planning. The objective of the workshop was to examine the role and relevance of manpower planning in the context of the shift towards market-oriented development policies and to ask whether there was a need for manpower planning and, if so, to suggest the form it should take.

As regards the *methodology* of manpower planning, the key question was whether there is a need to forecast the skill composition of employment and how useful attempts at this have been in the past. Without doubt, the past record of forecasting has often been one that produced erroneous numbers because of the faulty estimation of various parameters and elasticities. Furthermore, in certain ways the notion that forecasting could be useful was based on a misreading of the empirical evidence on how labour markets function. But is it still valid to ask what types of forecast should be made and how they should be used to guide policy? What types of data and research would be required to support such exercises?

On the *role of government*, the workshop set out to review government policies and interventions, to examine how useful manpower and human resource development plans have been and to ask what had been the impact of public sector employment policies on manpower allocation and development. To answer this, it is necessary to critically examine public sector training policies and the distortionary effects of related interventions. Policy lessons could be drawn from the results of "rate-of-return analysis" and "social cost-benefit analysis" of government intervention.

A further objective was to *identify* the types of *labour market analysis* required to support the formulation of manpower policies. These include, for example, the analysis of market and policy distortions, wage and salary structure, the policy environment and its impact on individual and enterprise decisions on training, the use of tracer studies and the analysis of hiring practices.

The workshop set out to answer these questions by looking both at the historical experience of manpower planning in selected countries and at more recent and more nuanced attempts to alert education and training systems to likely shifts in the pattern of demand for manpower. Many papers discussed the nature of available information on labour markets and the use which can be made of it.

A first conclusion of the workshop was that the old manpower projections approach to manpower planning is of limited value. However, in sectors and occupations where it is likely that a small number of highly skilled individuals would be needed in the future, some quantitative estimates remain necessary. A second conclusion was to support an improvement of labour market analysis in order to identify skill mismatch and labour underutilization. Better collection of wage data is an obvious first step, but information on productivity will also be needed.

Finally, the ILO was called upon to bring the discussions and conclusions of the workshop to a wider audience of Ministries of Labour, Ministries of Planning and other concerned ministries, as well as to other persons dealing with issues related to human resource development. I hope that this volume will reach that wider audience, and stimulate a further debate on the potential role of manpower planning, and its usefulness as well as its limitations.

J. Lönnroth,
Director,
Employment Department,
International Labour Office

Contents

Figure

Tables

1

Issues in manpower analysis

Peter Richards*

1. Introduction

It has been an article of faith in debates on development that by active intervention in the process of skill acquisition and labour allocation a government can accelerate the pace of output growth. According to that view, governments should see to it that talented people were educated and trained. The labour market, in terms of private sector methods of wage determination, and the individual process of occupational choice and mobility, was felt unlikely to do the job properly. Linked to this responsibility which governments were asked to accept has always been a number of unavoidable problems in allocating public education expenditure, between different education levels and between the competing claims of quality and quantity. The linkage cannot be avoided; decisions on the quality of primary education or the size of the secondary education sector inevitably affect the nature of training policies and skills development. The linkage also has significant associations with perpetuating or changing the pattern of income distribution and governments implicitly or explicitly take a stand on it. Although with the passage of time primary education has become nearly universal, the issue of whether to commit more resources to raise its quality is also practically universal.

Early attempts were made to put all these issues of education, training and labour allocation into perspective and, in a way, to solve them optimally by a mixed form of "manpower and educational planning". Soon it was clear that despite their substantive interaction, the institutions and instruments for manpower planning and educational planning were separate and likely to remain so. More recently it has also been realized that we have no means of resolving these issues; correspondingly more effort is now being made to cut the problems down to size and through manpower analysis to assess precisely what can or need be done, and by whom.

* International Labour Office.

2. Early approaches

In many developing countries, especially in the 1960s, the dilemma inherent in manpower and educational planning was viewed in terms of two major issues which were generally seen to be in conflict with each other. Much of the subsequent controversy surrounding manpower forecasting and other methods of manpower analysis has concerned means of resolving that conflict. One issue was the obvious need to raise the general education level of the population, prompted by both equity and efficiency concerns. The other was the, at least apparent, need to have the technically skilled people available to complement, and possibly to induce, investment in physical capital, usually in the context of an import-substitution strategy. To many observers in the late 1960s and early 1970s it seemed that for whatever reason the second objective was predominant and had led to the development and implementation of manpower plans based on forecasts of future skill needs. Governments may have made this choice because manpower forecasting appeared to have more scientific arguments on its side and to be an essential element of a strategy of industrial growth; however, it may have been that manpower forecasting effectively complemented a politically-inspired pattern of education expenditure which focused both quantitatively and qualitatively on secondary and higher education at the expense of primary.

Consequently, manpower forecasting and reliance on such forecasts to guide spending decisions began to be attacked from two angles. One argument was that such a form of planning gave information of a completely spurious reliability, because it was inherently difficult to forecast any distance into the future and because the possibilities of substitution between different categories of skilled and educated workers, in line with market-determined wage levels and labour costs, were being neglected. The other argument was that manpower planning was associated with a neglect of spending and research on improved primary education.[1]

Nearly 20 years back Mark Blaug noted that higher education had been the fastest-growing part of the educational system in very many developing countries and that the principal rationale for the rapid expansion of higher education had been manpower forecasting: with long-term manpower forecasts in Africa, Asia and Latin America foreseeing an enormous shortage of secondary and higher education manpower. In a study for the ILO he wrote, "In the last few years (i.e. the late 1960s), however, a sense of disillusionment with manpower forecasting had gradually spread through the world, in part because it implies an over-rigid view of the capacity of the economic system to absorb educated people into employment, and in part because of a growing fear that it constitutes an open-ended invitation to expand secondary and higher education without limits" (Blaug, 1974). He considered that some of the disillusionment was because manpower forecasting seemed to leave the educational planner with virtually no choices left to make. "The typical manpower forecast necessarily

---

[1] Manpower planning in terms of making, or using, forecasts is still widely practised, although with somewhat more caution than before. Whether, despite its drawbacks, manpower forecasting has generated better policies than reliance on intuition and guesswork would have done is an empirical question (Colclough, 1990). More complex models allowing for substitution between skills have been developed, e.g. the MACBETH model designed by Hopkins, Crouch and Moreland (1986).

commits the bulk of educational expenditures to the expansion of secondary and higher education. It is only after this first call on public funds is met that the educational planner can start thinking about such alternatives as quantitative expansion versus qualitative improvements, formal education in schools versus informal on-the-job training, and adult literacy versus schooling for children; but on all these questions he gets no help from manpower forecasts."

"In retrospect", Blaug continued, "it is easy to see why manpower forecasting enjoyed such popularity, and its intuitive appeal is such that it will probably endure for many years to come... Similarly, there has been some reluctance to accept the limited ability of economists to forecast the economic future accurately. Of course, no one is surprised to discover that completely accurate forecasting is impossible over such lengths of time (five to ten years); but what is disturbing is that virtually all manpower forecasts of the long-term variety have turned out to be seriously wrong."[2] Nonetheless, he believed that fairly accurate predictions could be made for two- to three-year periods, which would be useful for an "active manpower policy" and would provide information for training programmes, labour placement services, vocational guidance, etc.

The rate-of-return approach

The weapon wheeled out to overcome the alleged negative effects of manpower forecasting on the allocation of educational resources to the primary school sector was the "rate-of-return approach". In its early years of popularity this was used to demonstrate that primary education was a "better bet" than most other forms of education spending (and indeed than most other forms of investment) and as such its "power to move men's minds" by providing simple and apparently comparable statistics may have helped to meet certain equity objectives.[3] But one of the many problems associated with this kind of cost-benefit analysis was a neglect of external effects, since the only gains quantified were those accruing to the individuals who had received the education in question. Furthermore, rate-of-return analysis could shed no light on the extent to which households needed to be encouraged to undertake certain "human capital investments". Thus, for example, the persistence of primary school drop-outs coexisting with high private rates of return could be caused either by a family decision on the relative priorities of work or schooling, or by insufficient government resources devoted to primary education.

Furthermore, even within its own sphere the rate-of-return approach has drawbacks. It makes the very questionable basic assumptions that observed wages reflect the marginal product of labour, and that the content of the marginal years of

---

[2] This has been shown consistently (Hollister, 1967; Jolly and Colclough, 1972; Ahamad and Blaug, 1973; Amjad, 1987).

[3] Certain patterns can be drawn from an international comparison of results (see Psacharopulos et al., 1983). First, rates of return to investment in education are usually higher than for physical investment. Second, returns to education are higher in countries at a lower stage of development, and with a narrower base of education. Third, returns to primary education (whether social or private) are the highest among all educational levels.

schooling an individual undertakes is responsible for the marginal increase in his income. Calculations allowing for other forms of ability usually show lower rates of return. (For other methodological drawbacks see Behrman, 1990.) Also, while it provides an indication of the direction of future profitability, the rate-of-return approach does not provide quantitative estimates of the extent of the desirable expansion. In that sense it is not a complete substitute for the claims of the manpower forecasting approach. (The rate-of-return approach does, however, very usefully draw attention to the costs, as well as the benefits, of acquiring education and training.)

The existence of positive externalities, i.e. that in a market-based economic system, household and enterprise decisions on skill acquisition are likely to be suboptimal because the educated individuals cannot capture the gains which accrue to others, has long been recognized as a possibility. More recently attention has also been given to the issue of policy-based distortions, i.e. to asking whether household and enterprise decisions are being negatively biased by an inappropriate and publicly determined incentive structure. The last is naturally not always easy to define. The absence of a market for educational loans may have very major effects on household decisions to seek training; but it is not necessarily a distortion, in the sense of an outcome resulting from a policy decision. Nonetheless, certain intersectoral, interoccupational and intertemporal job and skill acquisition choices may well be biased one way or the other by government intervention in labour, and product markets, undertaken in pursuit of other objectives. Minimum wage legislation as an obstacle to enterprise level training effectively financed by the trainee is one such example. Trade protection may also have the effect of reducing training to below its optimal level.

3. Changing concepts of manpower analysis

But however manpower planning and analysis may have worked in the past, whether through anticipating a forecast demand for skills irrespective of market signals, or through determining rates of return to educational levels in order to make largely spurious comparisons both inter- and intra-sectorally, current thinking takes a different line. Corresponding to the increased emphasis put on market-oriented systems of resource allocation, current slogans in manpower analysis pinpoint such concepts as transparency in labour markets and reward systems, and flexibility of acquired education and training rather than numerical accuracy in forecasting. They also strongly play down the role of the government, and suggest especially that publicly subsidizing skill acquisition is not necessary.[4]

While this shift in thinking may well reflect a realization that economic systems are complex and cannot realistically be expected to be successfully manipulated from the centre, it is also probably true that over the past 30 years or so many economies have become more complex while more actors capable of intelligent decentralized decision-making have emerged. At the same time the very success of earlier educational programmes has raised the average education level of the labour

---

[4] cf. Behrman (1990): "while there is some evidence that human resources contribute to development in general and growth in particular, there is virtually no evidence that the social gains exceed the private gains".

force and, in large parts of the developing world, primary education is virtually universal. (There are some notable exceptions, e.g. Pakistan and Bangladesh.) On the one hand this last development has set aside part of the earlier debate on setting priorities between education sectors and has thus rendered some rate-of-return analysis nugatory. On the other hand, it may have helped to create conditions in which market liberalization was more likely to work.

Correspondingly the paradigm of manpower planning and analysis has changed, away from that of a factory manager who knows (or is told) he will need a certain number of technicians in a few years in order to cooperate with a determined level of technology, and is supplied with these workers fresh from training school to labour in that enterprise indefinitely. The current paradigm is of relatively short-term time horizons, of relative wages changing with demand and supply and of managers substituting technicians of one skill level for another in a flexible, and profit-maximizing manner. Both paradigms are extreme. Former centrally-planned economies certainly lived with labour turnover and labour upgrading. Jobs were not necessarily for life, nor could training be a one-off affair. The second paradigm implies a far more unsettled process of labour adjustment to skill needs than usually occurs. Wage differentials do not necessarily widen and contract in line with supply and demand.[5] Forecasting skill needs can occur without scarcities first having to arise. Wage determination also responds to comparability and seniority. Governments as employers are particularly affected by a difficulty in achieving a quick adjustment of relative pay so that occupational wages can easily vary between the government and the private sector.

The second paradigm does, however, implicitly accept that some traditional manpower planning questions cannot be answered because economic systems can adjust at different levels to different constraints. Thus there is no answer to the question of how many engineers or accountants a country needs. It is perfectly feasible to plot the numbers on a graph of countries ranked by per capita incomes but that tells what is, and how far individual countries stray from the trend line, not what should be. The simple answer is that a country needs as many of such skilled people as it can afford. If there are too many, their earnings will be too low to keep them in that occupation. If there are too few, then other subterfuges will be tried, e.g. using work-gang foremen to build roads instead of civil engineers.

It can be objected, as perhaps in the latter example, that markets can be relied on to allocate labour and determine levels of skills acquisition only up to the point where it becomes necessary or helpful for governments to set up programmes and make investments; at that stage opaque inertia sets in. This could be because governments are not profit maximizers and there is an apparent irreversibility of certain government agency functions. As a result bureaucracy may continue in perpetuity because of its immunity from market forces. Consequently treasuries often feel that if no government activities are going to contract none should expand. Thus an investment which a private agency might be willing to undertake may be only very reluctantly accepted by a government.

---

[5] It must also be accepted that, for a number of institutional and cultural reasons, workers do not always go where their private gains may appear to be highest (Rodgers, 1986).

The essence of a decentralized system of manpower development and skill acquisition is that the government's role is limited in favour of that of individual labour market actors. Reasoning would, however, suggest that individuals, households and enterprises do not always take socially optimal decisions.

One reason is that they are faced with a set of prices which itself results from forms of government intervention, e.g. in labour markets through wage legislation and controls, or in trade flows. Other government policies would change the forms of intervention and the relative prices facing these different actors, leading to their choosing more or fewer skills. A second complication concerns the inability of different sets of actors to trade current for future consumption on anything like the same terms. Some individuals can borrow money from banks to finance this training period, some from relatives, and some not at all. Enterprises face very similar problems. There is thus an issue of horizontal equity by which actors who are (fairly) certain of equal future income streams cannot borrow on the same terms and are subject to a form of random selection.

Reasoning would also suggest that the best decisions are likely to be taken when it is fairly clear what decisions are likely to be taken by all the other actors involved. Finally, even if no direct evidence is forthcoming, there will, no doubt, always be a feeling that correcting for factors which influence individual decisions is still not enough, because individuals, or enterprises, are not able to reap all the benefits which arise when they embody a new set of skills. The result is the very commonly held (but as noted far from universal) view that social gains from skill acquisition can, and do, outweigh private gains so that decisions taken purely on the basis of private calculation will result in an inappropriately low level of acquired skills. This is not an argument based on the fact of income inequality and the greater difficulty faced by the poor in financing an extended period of education and training. Even with perfect income equality it could still, in principle, be possible that the amount of training or education solicited by an individual or paid for by an enterprise was suboptimal. A manpower analyst thus needs to consider whether in any particular context the social benefits of skill acquisition exceed the private ones. At the extreme, does the participation of one more educated worker in a group of others raise the output of each and everyone with gains which cannot be attached by the more educated member? Can and should the government then tax away (most of) those windfall gains in order to subsidize the education and training of the more talented?

4. Government roles

This discussion suggests that in the "decentralized" paradigm the role of the government may be fivefold, namely (a) if it makes sense to do so, to correct for any distorting effects of its own policies on the conditions under which individual, including enterprise, decisions on skill acquisition and labour allocation are taken; (b) to increase the horizontal equity of access to finance; (c) to guide the skill acquisition process; (d) to increase the flexibility of its own "in-house" skill acquisition and labour allocation process; and (e) to take decisions on the relation of social to private benefits in this process and act upon them through expenditure and revenue decisions.

Compensating for policy-induced distortions

The decisions on skill acquisition which would result from the operation of market forces can be altered by government intervention in labour, commodity or financial markets. Governments can effectively change relative wages either directly, or indirectly, by changing the profitability of certain activities, production processes, etc. with subsequent effects on the demand for skills. Most such interventions were obviously undertaken in order to promote economic development and indeed to overcome perceived failures in the functioning of the markets. Furthermore, forms of government intervention aimed at accelerating growth would usually raise either the level of labour skills demanded, or the number of workers with a relatively high skill level. In such circumstances it would be incorrect to speak of a need to "compensate" for the effects of government policies on skill acquisition. However, a manpower analyst should be aware of the likely consequences for decisions on skill acquisition which would follow from significant changes in the pattern of government intervention.

It is more important, however, to identify where government intervention has the effect of reducing the demand for skill acquisition by individuals or enterprises and to propose remedial action. An obvious cause of concern would be policies and forms of wage control which effectively reduced wage differentials, perhaps through legislating and otherwise supporting a relatively high minimum wage level. Low wage differentials would then reduce the interest of individual workers in further skill acquisition, although they would not directly reduce the interest of enterprises in providing in-plant skill development. Naturally some such wage control action can be self-defeating, e.g. places in training establishments may not be filled up, shifts may occur towards occupations where wages are not controlled, or out of specialized activities into more general management. A further possible result of a high minimum wage is that remuneration could not be pushed down to a level where the worker effectively pays for enterprise specific on-the-job training at the beginning of his career. An enterprise might find, however, that if it was prevented from rewarding skilled labour sufficiently, it could not keep the people it trained. In that case there would be a argument for subsidizing enterprise training.

This discussion demonstrates how a different policy stance on labour market, especially wage, regulation or deregulation can easily change the pattern of skill development. However, unless overriding social considerations were involved, it would generally make little sense for a government aware of the consequences of its labour market regulation policies for skill acquisition to keep the policies in being and subsidize an alternative pattern of skill development, "as if" wages were fixed by the market. Above all, only by shifting to a market-based system will the deficiencies be revealed. Marginal fiscal tinkering is nonetheless always possible.

As noted, the form of government intervention in trade flows also necessarily has skill acquisition effects. No doubt a change in relative commodity prices towards trade liberalization will reduce the degree of protection given to certain activities and allow greater competition both from foreign final products and from new domestic producers. Greater competition will at least in part result in demands for higher quality outputs in both goods and services. In turn this will necessitate an upgrading of certain skills.[6] Similarly allowing foreign operation in the service sector and in manufacturing can easily have a "knock-on" effect, whereby local competitors are forced to pay more attention to staff quality. However, of course, it is one thing to speculate on how the skill acquisition and labour allocation process would change if the trade regime changes, and another to simulate an alternative set of skills without changing the trade regime. Furthermore, without an actual shift towards a more competitive environment it is doubtful if the quality effect of higher skill training would stick. In fact in low-income countries it also seems likely that at least initially trade liberalization will lead to some "deskilling" and a shift towards a lower skilled labour force, at least in manufacturing, as the pattern of manufacturing output changes.

Horizontal equity

The issue of moving closer to horizontal equity, whereby every investor in human capital, whether an individual or an enterprise, facing a similar stream of future earnings is able to find finance on the same terms, raises a number of issues. Banks are unwilling to provide such finance because an individual's future income stream is not only uncertain, but is based on no tangible and recoverable assets. Governments, however, can use income taxation precisely to cream off a part of the private return accruing to the more highly-educated and trained. Banks inevitably will favour households and indeed enterprises with their own assets. There is thus an argument for government intervention in aiding access to finance.

The issue of financing naturally raises the question whether an act of skill acquisition is comparable to any other form of investment and thus whether decisions on skill development are likely to be taken by comparing marginal productivity increases in a functioning labour market with an interest rate, set by the marginal productivity of capital. An enterprise might conceivably compare a decision to spend money on training with one of spending money on machinery, but in general the two would be complementary. The calculation of how much to spend on staff upgrading, irrespective of technology-imposed requirements, is no doubt a very difficult one to make in a scientific manner.

In 1973, the ILO employment mission to the Philippines made great play with the finding that while many private rates of return to education were relatively low, they were nonetheless higher than many "outsider" families could get in financial markets. Thus, under financially repressed conditions, education was a good investment despite some educated unemployment. But is there evidence that with a higher opportunity cost of money in the absence of financial repression, and with better savings facilities, families are less interested in educational spending?

Probably the answer is "no". Many countries in the 1980s have seen somewhat higher real interest rates than before (and possibly more reliable opportuni-

---

[6] The Pakistan Manpower Commission (1990) has argued that markets adjust to low skill levels by producing lower quality products, which then require international protection to be profitable.

ties for household savings), together with reduced public, and increased private, spending on education and a relatively poor outlook for real wages. If private rates of return to education have indeed fallen without the demand for education falling then it must be concluded that private education expenditure has a high consumption element. "Open", private sector based systems of secondary and higher education seem highly robust despite relatively low rates of return to those levels of education.

If this is so then capital market distortions may have little effect on household decisions on skill acquisition. Households will accept considerable sacrifices in order to acquire higher skill levels for their talented members. This may, however, only reinforce some of the problems of the absence of horizontal equity since the less talented may still be able to tap greater household savings. The compensating role of the government may nonetheless be narrowed.

Are such distortions in access to finance important in enterprise decisions or spending on training? If at the margin available funds are rationed by non-price means, it seems unlikely that borrowed money would be used for training expenses, rather than for, e.g., inventories. If all sources of capital were equally accessible, a relatively "unknown" activity like training might be more favoured. However, it may well be that the types of firms most likely to expand training are those which rely predominantly on internally generated funds for all kinds of expansion. Possibly the faster they expand the more they will train.

Guidance

A further role of the government within the decentralized paradigm of skill acquisition is to assist the various actors involved in making the best decisions possible. Two basic means apply: the dissemination of information and quality control. Even in a fully decentralized system of skill acquisition, providers of training cannot be infinitely flexible. To switch from offering one kind of training course to another requires the design of a new curriculum and probably retraining the training staff. Thus as in any business, forecasting is required of the likely demand for training by individuals or enterprises, at least over a period sufficiently long to cover those requirements. Certain types of skill development will take longer than others, particularly where new facilities have to be constructed and money to be borrowed. The necessary forecasting can and should, of course, begin by assessing market developments in terms of supply patterns reflected by wage changes.[7] However, the forecasting process, as noted, may be a deliberate attempt by employers to change the pattern of labour supply without disruptive effects on relative wages.

---

[7] Enterprise-level surveys are now being increasingly used to collect detailed information on the structure of the workforce by occupation and education, identifying occupations in which there are critical shortages, available training facilities, level of wages differentials and employee welfare benefits. Governments use such surveys to cover a wide cross-section of labour and employment issues including the debates on adjustment and labour flexibility (e.g. Standing (1990), on Malaysia) or monitoring the progress of labour market reforms (e.g. ARTEP (1988), on China).

That forecasting is essential in setting up training courses and facilities does not necessarily imply that governments must undertake it.[8] The principle of subsidiarity should be applied, i.e. decentralization to the lowest level possible. Governments are, however, uniquely placed to collect and analyse information at any geographical level and, of course, are in a position to change the pattern of labour demand by policy changes affecting forms of trade and labour market intervention. Thus the government can pass on to employers, and indeed make public in general, its assessment of where the economy is leading and which activities are likely to be favoured.[9] How that information is transformed by employers into a pattern of demand for skills depends on the changing size and technological nature of the capital stock. Such decisions are essentially to be taken at the decentralized level where all the various partial pieces of information can be collated.

It also seems likely that the government has a role to play in quality control. To some extent it is true that if employers are unhappy with the products of a particular training centre then competition among training producers will let a better training centre expand. It is also true that all purchasers do not demand the same quality product and that some employers will pay less for a less well-trained worker. Nonetheless, in some developing countries the market for skilled labour is so small that no competition can emerge among training providers. Furthermore there can be health and safety dangers in relying on very poorly trained workers who are unaware of how much they have not learned.

Government employment

A further point concerns the government as an employer. Since in very many countries the government is a major employer of skilled labour, the process by which skill acquisition takes place for public sector employees is important. Clearly the government hardly conforms to any decentralized paradigm. The government is essentially a unitary agent and to the extent that the government can be broken down into separate agencies, there is more rent-seeking rivalry than genuine competition between them. Price signals affecting career decisions which emerge from such rivalry may well be socially irrelevant. In addition government employment is generally of a lifetime nature with seniority having a major influence on wage developments. With a lifetime employment pattern the government cannot dismiss those with antiquated skills and hire those with more appropriate skills. As a result, government may well cling to antiquated and inefficient techniques and technologies because its skill pattern will lag behind that of more competitive agencies. The strong element of seniority in wage determination may also, after a while, reduce any individual inducement to acquire new skills.

---

[8] "Critical skills analysis" (whose methodology is spelled out by Hollister and Kam (1990), for Malaysia) assumes that employers do not have access to the same kind of information on the changing pattern of industrial production that the government has. Government therefore attempts to avoid labour market disruption by stockpiling labour with skills which will become "critical".

[9] Competent employers' organizations therefore need to be encouraged to develop and to pool their own labour market information.

However, no doubt governments vary greatly in their flexibility in the area of manpower allocation, whether by an ability to create new career paths, establish new earnings differentials or encourage new skill acquisition or to set up quasi-independent agencies to accomplish particular tasks with some freedom in wage setting. The issue can perhaps only be flagged here but a government manpower analyst should investigate it further.

Externalities

The last issue for consideration in manpower analysis is perhaps the most important one, namely to take a viewpoint in any particular context on what exactly counts as a positive or a negative externality in skill acquisition, to the extent that individual decisions taken with perfect foresight could still produce too little or, indeed, too much skill development. Of course, if education and training are pursued as desirable elements of consumption it is hard to conclude that they can be overdeveloped. And if someone trained in skill A ends up working with a related skill AB, that need not prove that investment in producing skill A was wasted. The individual may have felt inclined towards acquiring skill A and later exploited certain attributes of his instruction to carry out skill AB. (However, if training for skill A was highly subsidized and that for AB was not, then there could well be a social loss.) A more clear-cut example of a system which led to individuals choosing an excessive degree of education or training would be when acquiring a certificate of accomplishment was used mainly or solely as a device for rationing access to jobs – "credentialism". Where this happens it results in educational inflation, a drive to acquire higher than necessary education levels in order to out-compete rivals. It is generally associated with government employment, precisely because governments are not profit-seeking agencies.

Generally more attention is given to positive than to negative external economies.[10] This tendency has been identified by certain aspects of "new" growth theory which sees human resource development as contributing to a process whereby capital accumulation can lead to economies of scale and thus to divergence between the growth pattern of different countries and not the convergence that was forecast by neo-classical theory. However, new growth theory would generally place the emphasis in assessing the contribution of human resource development to growth in a high-level ability to introduce new products and processes by designing and redesigning machines. The availability of capable skilled labour working at internationally competitive productivity levels is not enough for sustained growth. Research and development teams are needed.

However, it is hard to see how many developing countries can fit into this model. Most basic research will be carried out in richer countries, most new product and process development will be undertaken by multinational corporations which may, in one way or another, secure its introduction into developing country markets

---

[10] cf. Romer's remark about the relation of education to economic outcomes that "the accumulated evidence suggests that education almost certainly has a causal role that is positive, but beyond that our knowledge is still uncomfortably imprecise" (Romer, 1989).

---

when they consider the time to be ripe. Conversely it should not be too difficult for some developing countries to "catch up" by copying existing processes. If this kind of work is not going on, the effects of education are "bounded" by the skills and experience of the individual worker, and human capital has no value beyond that of attracting multinational investment without any contribution to product and process development.

This may be a valuable insight and it may suggest that the most significant external economies are found at the higher university level so that a policy of individually-tailored subsidies, perhaps directed through potential employers, may be highly desirable.[11] But it sheds no light on the question of how wide the secondary school net should be cast in order to produce the candidates for such high-level training. Nor does it indicate whether improvements in primary school quality may not be indispensable in preparing the habits of mind which will later produce higher-level talent.

5. Summary

The important role of decentralized decision taking in the process of skill acquisition is being increasingly recognized. A corollary is that local-level actors, i.e. workers, employers and providers of training, should have the best possible access to the best possible information. To provide that information inevitably requires some assessment of future trends, an assessment which will require both forecasting and flexibility. The forecasting element can be assisted by the government, which is best placed to judge where the economy is heading and may indeed be intending to take policy steps to change that direction. Flexibility will require attention to market signals, particularly wage levels, which will act as signals to both jobseekers and training providers.

Correspondingly the pairing of forecasting and flexibility can be applied to the government's decisions on its own manpower needs and process of manpower development. In the public sector a lower level of flexibility – in relative wages or in skill substitution – may imply greater reliance on forecasting. However, efforts should probably be made to strengthen the former and reduce the latter.

On the major issue of externalities, however, and on the issue of how government action in the education and training fields can best "crowd in" private investment, there are encouraging lines of development. Most governments, however, are not well placed to analyse these issues and international agencies have a responsibility to help them to build a framework within which they can be clarified.

---

[11] A number of recent studies have advocated such an approach. These include Chowdhury, Islam and Kirkpatrick (1988) who argue for what they term "directive structural adjustment" which has active government policies to expand R and D and human resource investments in order to change comparative advantage towards higher technology and higher value-added products.

References

Ahamad, B. and M. Blaug. 1973. *The practice of manpower forecasting: A collection of case studies* (Amsterdam, Elsevier).

Amjad, R. 1987. *Human resource planning: The Asian experience* (New Delhi, ILO-ARTEP).

ARTEP. 1988. *Labour market reforms in China: Report on pilot manpower survey in Shashi City, Hubei Province* (New Delhi, ILO-ARTEP).

Behrman, J. R. 1990. *Human resource-led development? Review of issues and evidence* (New Delhi, ILO-ARTEP).

Blaug, M. 1974. *Education and the employment problem in developing countries* (Geneva, ILO).

Chowdhury A., I. Islam and C. Kirkpatrick. 1988. *Structural adjustment and human resource development in ASEAN* (New Delhi, ILO-ARTEP, HRD Working Paper).

Colclough, C. 1990. "How can the manpower planning debate be resolved?", in Amjad, Rashid et al. *Quantitative techniques in employment planning* (Geneva, ILO).

Government of Pakistan, 1990. *Report of the National Manpower Commission* (Islamabad).

Hollister, R, 1967. *Technical evaluation of the first stage of the Mediterranean Regional Project* (Paris, OECD).

Hollister, R. and Wong Poh Kam. 1990. *Analysis of markets for critical skills in Malaysia* (Kuala Lumpur, UNDP/ILO/EPU (restricted)).

Hopkins, M., L. Crouch and S. Moreland. 1986. *MACBETH: A model for forecasting population, education in manpower and employment, underemployment and unemployment*, WEP Research Working Paper series, "Aspects of labour market analysis and employment planning", No. 11 (Geneva, ILO).

International Labour Office. 1973. *Sharing in development in the Philippines* (Geneva).

Jolly, R. and C. Colclough. 1972. "African manpower plans: An evaluation", in *International Labour Review* (Geneva, ILO), 106:2-3, Aug.-Sep.

Psacharopoulos, G. et al. 1983. *Manpower issues in educational investment*. World Bank Staff Working Paper 624 (Washington, DC).

Rodgers, G. 1986. *Labour markets, labour processes and economic development: Some research issues*. WEP Working Paper series, "Aspects of labour market analysis" (Geneva, ILO).

Romer, P. M. 1989. *Human capital and growth: Theory and evidence*. Working Paper No. 3173, Working Paper series, National Bureau of Economic Research (Cambridge, Massachusetts).

Standing, G. 1990. *Adjustment and labour flexibility in Malaysian manufacturing* (Kuala Lumpur, UNDP/ILO/EPU (restricted)).

2

From manpower planning to labour market analysis

George Psacharopoulos*

1. Introduction

The art of manpower planning is certainly in disarray. After decades of manpower forecasting practice, the field has received repeated and sustained critiques (see Ahamad and Blaug, 1973, Psacharopoulos, 1984, Youdi and Hinchliffe, 1985, World Bank, 1991). Those still practising the art might be rightly confused as to the mandate, methodology and overall usefulness of what they are doing.

In this paper I review how conventional wisdom is changing fast in this field, and I suggest a shift from traditional, old-fashioned, blind-alley activities in the area of manpower planning towards a set of more promising venues in labour market analysis.

2. Do's and don'ts in labour market analysis

Table 2.1 presents a summary display of the points I want to make in this paper. A line-by-line explanation follows.

From planning to policy analysis

"Planning" is becoming a word to avoid. The optimism with the central planning of the post-World War II years has collapsed, as is evident from the respective economic performances of countries that attempted to plan (ranging from India to the Soviet Union), and of laissez-faire countries and areas such as the United States and Hong Kong. The same applies to manpower planning. In spite of the efforts of many countries to plan their manpower needs for the future, unemployment among school-leavers has become worse over the years. In fact such unemployment might have been lower if no attempt had ever been made at manpower forecasting.

The desire to forecast manpower needs in order to prevent bottlenecks or excess labour supply is highly intuitive and appears logical. Why then has man-

* World Bank, Washington, DC. The views expressed in this paper are those of the author and should not be attributed to the World Bank.

power planning failed? The reason has to be sought in the inability of human nature to fully anticipate future developments. Linear extrapolation of past trends regarding technological change are doomed to fail. In every aspect of life we operate under uncertainty. Such uncertainty is impossible to fully incorporate into manpower forecasts.

Looking at it from another viewpoint, what would be the state of a society where everything could be predicted? If forecasts in the area of technology were completely reliable, then anticipated developments would already be taken into account in the way people behave today; hence there would be no need to plan for the *future*. At the extreme, manpower planning would be valid only in a static and dictatorial society where, say, 1,000 electrical engineers would be produced in the year 1995 and ordered by decree to fill 1,000 electrical engineering slots, and remain there until year 2050 or the end of their productive life.

However, the future is not so clear-cut. Planners (of any kind, and not only of the manpower variety) forget that economic progress and societal well-being come from *unanticipated* changes in the way we do things (call it invention or innovation, if you wish). In the above example, by the year 2020 the economy may "need" more nuclear engineers, or engineers of a new form of energy unknown today. We do not have to look hard for examples of this kind. Who could have predicted just a few years ago the near-death of the mechanical clock and the "writer"? Although nobody planned for the creation of electronic clock makers or computer-literate typists, these skills sprang up overnight in the labour market because there was a demand for them.

As the keyword "planning" is out, "policy" and "analysis" have become keywords that are in. Policy has a more modest, short-term pretension than planning. It means that "given the uncertainty of the future, I will at least try to correct *current* manpower imbalances (however these are defined)" rather than "I will grandiosely bulldoze 1,000 electrical engineers into the middle of the next century". Historically, manpower planners have locked themselves into long-term time horizons which leave little room for flexibility. In contrast, labour market analysts are constantly adjusting short- and medium-term analyses to reflect changing conditions, while always keeping the long-term in mind. More to follow on policy, after we put to rest some additional old-fashioned concepts.

From manpower to labour force

Feminists may object to the notion of manpower and wish to replace it with something like womanpower or personpower. But beyond the literate accuracy of the word, there are deeper conceptual objections to the use of "manpower". These objections become more obvious when we attach a common qualifier found in many development plans – "high-level manpower". Such manpower, referring to those with higher qualifications and university degrees, restricts the manpower planning exercise to a tiny segment of the working population. Planning only for this segment tacitly means that those with lesser qualifications are excluded from the planning exercise and are not subject to its policy.

Table 2.1. Do's and don'ts in labour market analysis

Less emphasis on:	More emphasis on:
Planning	Analysis/policy making
Manpower	Labour force
Counting heads	Measuring wages
Firm labour surveys	Household surveys
Opinion surveys	Tracer studies
Occupational profile	Educational profile
Public sector only	Private and informal sector
Production efficiency only	Equity/poverty
Technical efficiency	Economic efficiency
Output-labour relationships	Cost-benefit analysis
Fixed wages	Flexible wages
Manpower needs	Labour supply and demand
Skill-specific training	General training
School-based training	Firm-based training
Free-education/training	Cost recovery/user fees
Public education/training	Private education/training
Filling long-term skill gaps	Correcting present labour market distortions

This has been one of the most serious mistakes of manpower forecasting. It was thought that persons with less than a university education were in abundant supply, and hence there was no need to plan for them. This disastrous omission led to the creation of redbrick universities in Africa, in the midst of illiteracy of the majority of the population. Evidence supporting extensive primary education (for example, that farmers with even four years of education, other things being equal, produce more rice relative to farmers with no education) was not yet available (see Jamison and Lau, 1982). But even after such evidence became available, how many manpower planners have altered their approach?

As "manpower" is being phased out, "labour force" is emerging to the forefront. Labour force is a much wider concept than manpower. It includes the unemployed, and it leads to an examination of the reasons why some people are out of work. It ushers in many subtle analyses, as explained later in this paper, that go beyond what can be achieved with manpower forecasting.

From headcount to wage measuring

Manpower planning typically deals with headcount imbalances. For example, if it is projected that a school system will produce only 800 electrical engineers by the year 2050, whereas the country's production goals for that year imply the need for 1,000 engineers, a gap of 200 has to be filled. The naïveness of this argument is demonstrated by visiting a country where there is an alleged shortage of electrical engineers. Generally, this shortage pertains only to the public sector, where pay scales and salary limitations do not make it attractive to engineers to work for the State. By contrast, private and/or multinational companies operating in the country usually experience no shortage of engineers for the simple reason that they pay much higher salaries than the public sector.

A key set of statistics in labour market analysis is the wages and salaries of labour with different qualifications. Labour market analysis does not limit itself to headcounts, as manpower planning does. In labour economics, contrary to manpower planning, one cannot deal only with the physical quantity of different kinds of labour without attaching a price to it. Once prices are introduced, quantities become more "elastic", i.e. they change depending on the offered wage. To follow our example, if public sector wages were higher, the supply of electrical engineers would increase *without anyone having planned* for such increase. If the country's school capacity is limited at present to produce the extra engineers, such persons may come from abroad, be brought in from other occupations, or be trained on the job. On the demand side, a lower salary may mean a higher absorption of engineers, while a higher salary may mean unemployed engineers.

From firm employment surveys to household surveys

The statistical data used in manpower planning typically comes from the employment sector of the economy. This approach has the serious limitation that, in developing countries today, only a small fraction of the population works in modern establishments. Most work is in the agricultural and informal sectors of the economy. Therefore the majority of the labour force is ignored even before the manpower planning exercise begins. How effective is a manpower plan that starts with labour input-output coefficients based only on the public sector and/or organized employment? And who said that the present use of labour by the public sector is efficient and that its "needs" must be extrapolated into the future?

For effective labour market analysis and policymaking, the information must start from where labour is located, including the unemployed. The best place to obtain this information is in the household. Any other sample designed to study labour market issues is bound to be highly biased. Fortunately, household surveys are proliferating around the world and the data raised by them is being used for labour market analysis (e.g. see Grosh, 1990, for an example of the use of such data from the World Bank's Living Standards Survey).

From opinion surveys to tracer studies

Given the impasse which hindered early mechanical manpower forecasts, practitioners have resorted to so-called "key informants". These are people who are supposed to know a particular sector inside-out, e.g. the petrochemical industry, and thus are able to offer a judgement as to what types of skills the industry will need in the years ahead.

Although the information provided by these people has been far superior to the numbers resulting from mechanical manpower forecasts of the traditional kind, the fact remains that the information they provide is based on their opinion. It does not, and cannot, represent an exact description of hard facts about the future.

It might be better to base labour market policy on hard historical facts, rather than personal opinions about the future. One tool used extensively in labour market analysis by economists (but usually not by manpower planners) is the tracer study. This type of study follows a cohort of students, say of the faculty of electrical engineering, through graduation and a few years into the labour market. (See Psacharopoulos and Hinchliffe, 1983, and for a practical application Psacharopoulos and Loxley, 1985). By means of base and follow-up questionnaires, a tracer study records information about the students' personal and family characteristics, the length of time it took each student to obtain employment (if employed at all), the nature of the job landed (electrical engineering or cab driving?), earnings at the hiring point and earnings several years after graduation.

Given the impossibility of predicting the future, tracer studies are based on the philosophy that history repeats itself; policymaking can then take these historical tendencies into account. For example, if 20 per cent of graduates of the electrical engineering faculty for three successive years take two years to find a job, or if they enter occupations other than electrical engineering, these are signals of a slack in the market for electrical engineers. Although we do not know precisely what the market will be in five years time, perhaps admissions to the electrical engineering faculty should be reduced.

Indeed, manpower planning is also based on the historical relationship between output and labour – the so-called labour utilization coefficients (see Psacharopoulos, 1987). But contrary to the information provided by tracer studies, the fixed coefficients in manpower planning are extrapolated decades ahead. Moreover, they cannot be used to correct labour imbalances at the margin (more on this notion later).

From occupational categories to educational profiles

Manpower planning typically starts with a classification of the labour force by occupational category. Occupational classifications have ranged from one-digit (as in the early work of the OECD on the subject, see OECD, 1970) to four-digit occupational groups. For those who have not dug into the International Standard Classification of Occupations (ISCO, see ILO, 1990), they are reminded that a four-digit occupational code classifies job positions down to the level of "animal trainers or elephant drivers" (ISCO code 9332). It even differentiates "astrologers" (ISCO code 5151) from "fortune tellers" (ISCO code 5152). Each of these occupations is then translated into an educational profile which corresponds to that particular occupation. Setting astrologers aside, and following our example of engineers, such translations would apparently be easy if a one-to-one correspondence is assumed between a mechanical engineer and a graduate of the mechanical engineering faculty of the university.

There are at least two problems with this approach. First, there are many less clear-cut occupations, such as "middle-level technician", that do not correspond to a particular educational level. Even in the case of electrical engineers, such persons could come from a two-year rather than a four-year college, or have been trained on the job. They even could have been imported from abroad with no implications for the capacity of the country's electrical engineering faculty whatsoever.

The second problem is that "occupation", in and of itself, is not a policy variable. Analysis should be conducted in terms of potential instruments of policy. For example, you can have a policy of selectively expanding or contracting admissions to a secondary vocational school. But you cannot plan in terms of "executive and administrative workers" (What is/should be their educational background? Can these positions actually be "planned" for?).

It is for this reason that current labour market analysis focuses on the educational profile of the worker, rather than on his or her occupation. The results of labour market analysis using education as a classification criterion lead directly to policies on schools and universities. An occupational taxonomy, on the other hand, is nearly policy void. However, it is useful for other purposes (i.e. male-female dissimilarities in employment, gender discrimination).

From the public sector to private and informal employment

One famous joke about economists is that they have a tendency to look where the light is, not where the keys are lost. Manpower planners fit this description as well. Labour utilization coefficients, which are the basis of a typical manpower forecasting exercise were (and still are in some cases) derived by observing the number of workers per occupational/skill category in government employment or parastatal firms. If the private sector is also included, then observations are typically confined to large firms. The reason for this is that collection of such data is easy because of the concentration of workers in these environments.

However, the majority of workers in developing countries are found in "small firm" private employment or the ever-growing informal sector. These people are not generally included in manpower planning exercises. True, collection of data on such people is not easy and requires a household survey, as noted above. Even a street survey would be deficient since it would omit those who, for whatever reason, cannot make it to the street on the particular day of the survey. But the information gained through a household survey will dramatically enhance the ability of labour market analysts to develop effective policy recommendations for all sectors of the labour market.

A typical error in imitation "labour market analysis" is to observe workers' performance in firms and relate this performance directly to the educational background of the worker. For example, if the worker has a vocational secondary school background and performs well according to the supervisor's opinion, the manpower planner may jump to the policy conclusion that the country should produce more secondary vocational school graduates. What the planner might miss in this case is the fact that only five persons out of a class of 100 secondary vocational graduates entered employment directly after school (the rest attempting to enter the university system), and that out of these five only two entered an occupation that related to the vocation they learned in secondary school (the other three becoming clerks and one being unemployed).

Again, the answer regarding data collection for rigorous labour market analysis is a household survey or a tracer study. There is simply no substitute for them.

From production efficiency to poverty and equity

The archetypical manpower planner is obsessed with production efficiency: You must have so many skilled workers of a particular type for your future production to materialize. Theoretically this approach might appear sensible but there are two major problems with the way this approach has been applied in manpower planning.

First, the wrong type of efficiency might be used, and this is elaborated in the following subsection. Second, times have changed and efficiency is no longer the only criterion of social action – equity and poverty considerations are increasingly being taken into account when making labour market policy. For example, in some instances, the policymaker may promote labour-intensive technologies so as to boost employment and increase the share of labour in the national income, even though such technologies might not be optimal from the efficiency viewpoint.

From technical efficiency to economic efficiency

Sticking to the efficiency criterion, manpower planners typically mean *technical* efficiency, i.e. the best technical way of producing a particular product. By contrast, labour market analysts consider *economic* efficiency, i.e. they modify the input mix provided by the mechanical engineers according to the unit cost of the particular inputs. Thus, in some cases it might be economically more efficient to have a ratio of ten nurses to one doctor in order to provide a given level of health care to the population, although from a technical efficiency viewpoint the ratio should be five nurses to one doctor. Economic efficiency is arrived at by bringing prices into the analysis (in this case the relative salaries of doctors and nurses.) But, as explained above, prices are absent from a typical manpower planning exercise. Everything is counted in terms of doctors' and nurses' heads.

From output-labour relationships to cost-benefit analysis

This is an alternative way of expressing the point made above. Manpower planning is based on the relationship between output (expressed in physical or monetary terms) and the quantity of labour by skill educational level "required" for the production of such output. It makes no attempt to assess the economics of the contemplated action. Manpower forecasts usually end up being Rolls Royce solutions, typically choosing the best technical way to move from place A to place B.

By contrast, a labour market analyst includes the *cost* implications of increasing the supply of skilled labour by means of education/training type X or Y, and may end up with a Volkswagen solution for going from place A to place B.

From fixed wages to flexible wages

By ignoring wages, manpower planning tacitly assumes that such wages are fixed, or at least that they do not impact which skills are "needed" for the future. In contrast, the level of wages and salaries by skill/educational level is one of the main variables with which the labour market analyst will work. Wages influence both the demand for labour by employing firms, and the supply of such labour by individual workers. Ignoring the level and change of wages over time can only result in manpower forecasting of the crudest type.

It is for the same reason that no economist will ever use the word "need" in the context of labour market analysis. "Demand", yes. For there is always a price at which there will be no demand for a good or service, just as demand will increase as prices are lowered. "Need" is a subjective, absolute concept to be avoided, whereas labour supply and demand are relative and more rigorous concepts.

Skill-specific training versus general training

Due to the nature of the exercise, manpower forecasts typically result in recommendations for increasing the supply of labour with vocational/technical qualifications. But this merely extrapolates today's observed relationship between output and employment, without taking into account the future dynamics of the economy. However, from a labour analyst's perspective, it might be preferable to enhance the general competencies of the population, rather than lock a given cohort into a narrow, blind-alley occupation.

Today, it is increasingly recognized that general training, i.e. that which enhances the overall competencies of the trainee, is more cost-effective and safer in the long run than narrow vocational training. Recently, the United States Department of Labour (1991) published a report on what secondary school children should be taught in order to be prepared for the workplace. According to the report, graduates should be proficient in "five competencies", where technological ability comes last:

1. The ability to allocate resources
2. The development of interpersonal skills
3. The ability to assess information
4. The ability to understand work systems
5. The ability to deal with new technology.

From school-based training to firm-based training

The extrapolation of "necessary school output" from "needed occupational skills" is the bottom line of typical manpower forecasting. But even after we agree on the method of manpower forecasting or, preferably, labour market analysis, there is no reason why all specialized technicians would have to be produced in the country's formal school system.

The labour analyst, instead, will consider alternative ways of increasing the supply of such technicians. One way, which does not involve formal schools or training institutions of any kind, might be to deregulate the wage structure of technicians so that more people from the existing labour pool (now doing another kind of job) are drawn into this occupation. A typical example of this case is when the public sector complains about the scarcity of skill A. Before producing new graduates of type A, an increase in the salary of people who already possess skill A (well above the maximum set by the civil service pay structure) will almost certainly fill the Government vacancies in such skills overnight.

A second way of increasing the supply of the desired skills might be through the development of specialized vocational institutions which are *outside* the formal school system. Technical/vocational training within the formal school system has proved doubtful. Schools cannot follow the latest technology. Equipment remains unutilized and not maintained. Instead, dedicated vocational schools are better geared to market demands and are more likely to offer cost-effective education to the trainees.

Still, a far better way to achieve "relevance of the curriculum" and enhance "links between training and the labour market" is on-the-job training. Firms know better than any other entity what the latest technology is, and they can anticipate their demand for specific skills. The training they offer is not only likely to be efficient, but is also partly financed by the firm. Moreover, it keeps the worker employed while he/she is being trained, although at reduced wages (see World Bank, 1991).

From free education and training to cost-recovery

By virtue of not considering costs, the manpower planner tacitly assumes that the trainee or his/her firm will not pay for the training. Instead such training is paid for by the invisible taxpayer, and education and training become "free" goods. It is also politically popular (particularly with the middle and upper classes) to provide items such as education and training free of charge to the user.

Instead, the labour market analyst will try to find ways to explicitly shift at least some of the cost of training from the general taxpayer to the direct beneficiaries. This is not because the labour market analyst does not care about the poor. On the contrary, fee paying by students of high-income families is an equitable measure because it will mean more public resources are available to give fellowships to students of low income families. Also, fee paying enhances student selection and hence the efficiency of a university system. It allows more public resources to be channelled to the lower levels of education where the priority for educational expansion still lies in developing countries. (For an elaboration of these points see Psacharopoulos, Tan and Jiménez, 1986.)

From public education and training to private institutions

Typical manpower planning ignores not only the private sector as a source of labour demand, but also as a potential provider of education and training. The tradition has been to delegate to the public sector the creation of the country's qualified manpower.

But the labour market analyst will attempt to encourage the development of private training institutions to the extent possible. This is for reasons of efficiency and, paradoxically, equity. Private institutions operating under a profit motive are bound to be more cost-conscious relative to non-profit institutions. Since they have to survive on revenue from students, accountability passes from a remote central Ministry to the students' feet. If these students feel that the education or training they receive is not good or "relevant", they will stop attending and the institution will be obliged to close – or give way to a more efficient one.

Private training institutions also enhance the equity of the system as they allow more public resources to be concentrated on those students who have fewer financial means. User fees and tuition payments release part of the public education/training budget to be targeted more equitably on students from lower income families.

Of course, one special case of private institution training is on-the-job training. In such cases the cost of training is shared by the firm and the trainee himself/herself in the form of reduced wages while being trained.

From filling long-term skill gaps to correcting labour market distortions

This is one of the most fundamental differences between manpower planning and labour market analysis. The horizon of the manpower planner is long. The prime concern is to close an anticipated difference between the spontaneous supply of skills and the need for such skills by the economy. The horizon can sometimes be as long as 20 years.

By contrast, the labour market analyst has a much shorter horizon. The concern is with correcting present imbalances in the labour market, e.g. removing wage ceilings so that more persons of a particular skill offer themselves for employment, or even removing wage floors (such as the minimum wage) in order to allow more youth to be employed.

The typical manpower planner's approach is lump sum, jumpy and discontinuous, while that of the labour market analyst is gradual and marginal. Such analysts recommend gradual changes in the desired direction, then reassess the situation after a few months/years in order to take corrective action again. The future's uncertainty is recognized so there is no lock into a long-term "manpower development plan".

3. Concluding comments

Given the contrast between the old manpower forecasting technique and the newer labour market approach as described above, one may wonder why manpower forecasting activity has not completely subsided. In my opinion, the answer has to be found in human inertia. Economists are not the only ones who sometimes look where the light is, and not where the keys are lost. The remaining trace of popularity with manpower forecasting lies in its administrative appeal. After all, this is not the only activity which has maintained itself in society despite the abundance of more intelligent approaches to a situation.

References

Ahamad, B. and M. Blaug. 1973. *The practice of manpower forecasting: A collection of case studies* (Amsterdam, Elsevier).

Grosh, M. 1991. *The household survey as a tool for policy change* (World Bank, Living Standards Measurement Study, Working Paper No. 40).

Hinchliffe, K. and R. Youdi (eds.). 1985. *The practice of manpower forecasting revisited* (Paris, UNESCO, International Institute of Educational Planning).

International Labour Office. 1990. *International Standard Classification of Occupations: ISCO-88* (Geneva, ILO).

Jamison, D. and L. Lau. 1982. *Farmer education and farm efficiency* (Baltimore, Maryland, Johns Hopkins University Press).

OECD. 1970. *Occupational and educational structures of the labour force and levels of economic development* (Paris, OECD).

Psacharopoulos, G. and K. Hinchliffe. 1983. *Tracer study guidelines* (Education Department, World Bank (processed)).

Psacharopoulos, G. 1984. "Assessing training priorities in developing countries: Current practice and possible alternatives", in *International Labour Review* (Geneva, ILO), 123(5), 569-583.

Psacharopoulos, G. and W. Loxley. 1985. *Diversified secondary education and development: Evidence from Colombia and Tanzania* (Baltimore, Maryland, Johns Hopkins University Press).

Psacharopoulos, G., J-P. Tan, and E. Jiménez. 1986. *Financing education in developing countries* (Washington, DC, World Bank).

Psacharopoulos, G. 1987. "The manpower requirements approach", in G. Psacharopoulos (ed.). *Economics of education: Research and studies* (Oxford, Pergamon Press).

United States Department of Labor. 1991. *What work requires of schools: A SCANS report for America 2000* (Washington, DC: USDL).

World Bank. 1991. *Vocational and technical education and training: A policy paper* (Washington, DC).

3

Manpower planning and economic development

Robert E.B. Lucas*

1. Introduction

Four major themes are addressed in this paper. Section 2 discusses the problem of matching demand and supply for skills and the broad role of manpower planning in this process. Section 3 then addresses a number of reasons for state intervention in this process of skill matching, both for reasons of efficiency and of equality. Section 4 outlines the interconnections between skills, trade and development strategy, both in the context of static comparative advantage and in a dynamic, changing world, and Section 5 considers some of the policy instruments in common use in promoting or adjusting skill generation.

2. Matching demand and supply for skills

Manpower planning is commonly perceived as a public sector activity, but in fact the corporate sector undertakes a good deal of manpower analysis in its own interests. In determining a hiring strategy, corporations must (more or less formally) determine their occupational/skill needs. Whether this represents purely short-term needs or involves a longer-term view depends upon the firm's willingness to adjust the composition of labour force through retrenchment and hiring. The extent of commitment to a long-term association with specific workers, and hence the need for longer term formulation of manpower needs, varies considerably from firm to firm, depending in part upon size of the firm, stability of the industry and perhaps the cultural environment, as well as upon any job security legislation. Similarly, in deciding the extent and composition of training in which a firm is willing to invest, implicit or explicit manpower requirement projections must be undertaken within the private sector.

In parallel, state planning bodies in many countries (and not just in economies perceived as less market oriented) also undertake manpower requirement projections. These projections of demand normally encompass the public sector's own hiring plans but may also include projections for the private sector.

* University of Boston, Boston, Massachusetts.

As a planning tool, state manpower planning thus projects demands with the purpose of matching supply to these demands to avoid shortages. Supply is fitted to demand. In this extreme form, demands for specific skills are considered to be independent of their supply. In other words, the costs of hiring persons in a particular skill category do not enter the calculations. It is well known that this requires some very strong assumptions. The skill mix required for a certain level of output by an industry must be independent of the relative costs of those skills. In addition, the output mix both within and across industries must be independent of the cost of skills required in production. Whether these conditions are even approximately filled may well be doubted.

More satisfactory planning approaches can be envisioned and are occasionally implemented. Such models recognize the interaction between skill category supply and demand through a pricing mechanism, perhaps even incorporating some general equilibrium ramifications of this matching. At least implicitly, such cost considerations presumably do enter the manpower decisions of private firms. But if markets can clear the balance between the demand and supply for skills why is any state manpower planning necessary?

3. Reasons for state intervention in skill generation

In any context, the importance of state intervention in a set of markets may stem either from efficiency considerations or from concerns with respect to equality of opportunities or outcomes. These two will therefore be taken up in turn.

Efficiency considerations

Any positive externalities associated with education and skill acquisition render private decisions with respect to training investments err towards too little investment relative to the social optimum. Perhaps the most common sphere in which such positive externalities are discussed is with respect to basic education.

An educated population may take decisions which benefit others in a number of dimensions not reflected in any pricing mechanisms: educated women typically exhibit lower fertility rates, leading to less crowding; education may promote a better understanding of hygiene and health care, resulting in diminished dissemination of diseases; educated voters may be able to make better informed electoral decisions; and enhanced participation in cultural affairs by the better educated may be deemed a benefit, at least amongst the élite.

Positive externalities may also stem from the role of education in promoting national unity through common learning and language, and through promotion of specific ethical and perhaps religious values.

But any context where higher skills do not receive proportionate remuneration allows rents to be reaped by others, whether following formal education or other forms of training. In the context of the brain-drain, for instance, it is frequently maintained that doctors, nurses and teachers are not paid in proportion to

their contribution to the social well-being, leading to an under-investment in acquisition of these specific skills.

Signalling theory, on the other hand, hypothesizes an over-investment in
education. The source of the market "failure" in this case is an asymmetry in information between potential workers and employers with respect to innate aptitudes.
According to this view, individuals invest in their education to signal a high level of
potential which they believe they already possess. Since education then merely signals this preexisting potential without enhancing it, the result is an over-investment in
signalling. Yet it is far from clear that all signalling is wasted: for some employers it
may be crucial to select individuals with particularly high innate abilities, and signals
may then play an important sorting role.

Other asymmetries in information may also lead to inefficient private decisions. In particular, the rewards to investments in education and training are typically reaped over a protracted period. Individual persons have very limited information on which to form their expectations about future directions the economy is
likely to take and hence the future demands for specific skills. Firms also possess
limited information with respect to future market conditions and hence their long-
term demands for skills. Whether this limited information causes the market to fail
to generate efficient decisions with respect to skill investments is, however, con-
tentious. Information gathering is expensive. To plan on the basis of limited information is therefore not necessarily inefficient. Nonetheless, if the State genuinely
possesses more complete information about future conditions (over which they
exert some control), and is either unwilling or unable to disseminate this information to the public, then a case can be made for state intervention in guiding skill
acquisition founded on their better information.

Since training and education are clearly investments, often subject to long
gestation periods, one of the most important sources for market failure in matching
demands and supplies for skills arises in the financing of these investments. Human
capital does not offer collateral – certainly not before it is accumulated but not after-
wards either. As a result it can be difficult for individuals to borrow from private
sources to invest in the direct and indirect costs (from foregone earnings) inherent
in education and even on-the-job training. Employers are better able to raise capital
to invest in training. But employers are understandably reluctant to invest in general
training when trained employees may subsequently be poached by competitors. In
principle the problem of poaching can be addressed through long-term contracts,
though there are questions as to whether these contracts can always be enforced. In
addition, both individuals and firms may underinvest, both in physical and human
capital, if their private rate of discount is higher than the social rate. Whether this is
the case may be disputed; it would seem that pressures from financial markets may
be forcing producers in some Western economies to adopt a myopic position, but
elected governments do not always take a healthy long-run view either as elections
draw near.

A further, important element which may lead to socially inappropriate training decisions by private individuals and firms is a wage which fails to reflect the true
cost of labour. A wage for a particular skill or education level which is maintained
above market clearing may lead either to too little or too much investment in acquir-

ing this specific form of skill; this depends upon attitudes towards risk and upon who is paying for the training. Wages above true cost do presumably discourage employers from investing in training. Similarly, if artificially high wages result in unemployment an individual must weigh the chances of obtaining a well-paid job in deciding upon a career: if the individual is very risk-averse this may result in suboptimal training. On the other hand, if artificially high wages are accompanied by very little unemployment, incentives for excessive training on behalf of individuals are clearly established. A specific example of the last category arises when government acts as employer of last resort for graduates of higher education, perhaps fearing the political consequences of pay cuts or open unemployment among the educated: such action clearly establishes an incentive for individuals to continue their education beyond a level which may be socially efficient.

Considerations of equality

In the long run, the distribution of earnings among individuals is one of the most powerful determinants of the size distribution of incomes. In turn, education and training appear to be major factors in explaining the spread in earnings among individuals. As a result, policies to offer better access or opportunities for education and training among the poor and disadvantaged are appropriately viewed as potentially powerful tools in reshaping equality of incomes.

There are several reasons why being poor gives rise to lower rates of education and training, and the distinction between these has some importance in policy determination. First, the opportunity cost of funds for investment in education or training may well be greater for the poor – if only because they lack collateral. Second, poor people tend to live together, both in the sense of neighbourhoods and in broader regional terms. When the quality of schooling depends upon local finance and upon parental involvement, living in a poor area can mean poor quality schooling. Third, success in education of children depends upon early training at home and upon the attitudes of parents toward education. Poor parents are normally less well educated and consequently less well informed about educational opportunities and less well placed to offer support to their offspring in early training.

Even if more equal opportunity for a good education is offered, through scholarships and loans and a more even distribution of quality in schools, the outcome may still remain unequal as a result of such factors as the role of early parental input. Equal opportunity and equal outcome are not synonymous.

There are then a number of quite legitimate reasons for the State to want to intervene in the market for skill generation, both for micro-economic reasons of efficiency and because of the central role of training in affecting the distribution of incomes. Are there additional reasons for state intervention associated with macro-economic development strategies?

4. Skills, comparative advantage and development strategy

On the whole the answer is "no". However, in at least three ways the dynamics of human capital accumulation and development strategy are closely intertwined and these warrant some discussion before proceeding to consider policies with regard to skill generation in Section 5.

Multiple steady state growth paths

When externalities are important, the steady state path for equilibrium growth may not be unique. Since education in particular is thought to offer a variety of positive externalities, as discussed in the previous section, human capital has come to play a central role in the recent revival of interest in growth theory surrounding this phenomenon. There may be several equilibrium growth paths each consistent with a clearing market for skills though differing in income levels. When this is true, which market solution prevails is not a matter of indifference. Naturally there is an interest in achieving that path associated with the highest income levels. However, in policy terms this appears to involve little more than taking appropriate account of any externalities inherent in education, raising no additional concerns.

Comparative advantage and infant industries

The Leontief paradox refers to a finding that the United States actually exports relatively labour intensive products, in part because American labour is (or at least used to be) more highly trained than in competing nations. At least since the isolation of the Leontief paradox the importance of skill and training in defining comparative advantage in international trade has come to the fore. An abundant supply of trained labour tends to establish a comparative advantage in producing skill-intensive products and hence being able to export these goods to less well-trained nations.

This has led some policymakers to think of the corollary – to invest in training in order to establish a comparative advantage in skill-intensive products. But do skill-intensive products and processes deserve special attention ?

The arguments are essentially the same as those associated with infant industries. Many countries have protected capital-intensive infant industries in order to develop a comparative advantage in heavy industries. In a few instances this has been successful though often at considerable cost. More often the infants never grow up.

It is now well understood that any legitimate reasons for wanting to help infant industries involve either some form of dynamic externality, such as free learning by one firm from the costly experiences of another, or they involve capital market failures limiting investment in physical or human capital. In neither case is the best form of response one of import protection. But since either learning or training lies at the heart of these concerns, the focus has shifted to high-tech industries and away from the capital-intensive smokestack industries. Naturally there is considerable danger that countries bent on protecting their high-tech industries will simply make the same mistakes as many which protected the capital-intensive infants in the past: the high-tech infants may fail to become competitive exporters.

Yet there are countries which have been more successful with their infant industries. The newly industrializing countries of East Asia have hardly been paragons of laissez-faire; they have often successfully identified and supported infant industries. Some studies suggest that one reason that the East Asian economies may have been more successful in their dynamic strategy resides in the simultaneous development of a skilled labour force able to turn the infant industries into successful exporters. Many foreign technologies cannot simply be imported and installed in turnkey projects: they require not only a skilled labour force to operate them but also require adaptation to local settings and this requires skills both of management and workers.

To sum up, a case can be made for training deliberately to establish a comparative advantage in an associated industry. This may either be justified on the grounds of externalities and hence achieving a higher equilibrium growth trajectory, or on more traditional infant industry grounds of capital market failures or learning externalities and hence insufficient training. Some countries appear to have been successful in pursuing such a strategy. But it is also a risky strategy with potentially high costs, as many countries which have promoted infant industries in the past have discovered. The reasons for success in a few countries in identifying appropriate infants and training accordingly, while the majority of countries make costly mistakes in this sphere, are not well understood. Two possible factors may, however, be tentatively suggested. The first is the synergy between related industries, so that successful infants may occur in lines closely related in production and marketing terms to product lines in which a competitive advantage is already well established. The second is the apparent critical role played by the private sector both in helping to design the development strategy and in formulating and even conducting the associated training in successful contexts. The latter is a theme to which Section 5 will return.

Evolving comparative advantage: The need for flexibility

The third line of argument to be mentioned here is the state of flux which can prevail in a dynamic global setting. The range of industries in which an economy has a comparative advantage can shift substantially over time. This may be a result of altered endowments within the specific country itself. But it may also reflect factors external to this country. Patterns of world demand change through time. So does the state of know-how. Today's high-tech industries are tomorrow's standardized processes (as in electronics assembly); today's labour-intensive industries can also be tomorrow's frontiers (as in robotized textiles). In such a world it is very difficult to forecast with any accuracy the future set of industries in which a country is likely to be competitive. Yet it is on such forecasts which manpower planning relies. This state of flux has profound implications for the appropriate design of a manpower strategy – implications which will be discussed in the context of policy in the following section.

5. Policy instruments and decisions in skill generation

In working toward more equal opportunities in education and training, perhaps in striving for more equal outcomes, in attempting to improve on the efficiency of decisions with respect to skill acquisition, perhaps in association with the design of a dynamic development strategy, there are a number of quite legitimate reasons for wanting to intervene in the private market for training. But what forms might these interventions take?

As a general principle, it is most effective to deploy a policy instrument which acts as directly as possible upon the perceived problem. In practice, a broad distinction may be made between the role of the State in offering financial incentives and support in education and training, and in the role of the State as provider of training, though of course the two often overlap. No matter whether policymakers are deciding how much to spend upon primary versus tertiary education, deciding how many scholarships to offer for engineering versus arts students, deciding on the syllabus and vocational content in schooling, or deciding upon courses to offer in public training establishments, they are effectively undertaking manpower planning in some form. What are some of the issues and alternatives?

Financing education

One of the principal market "failures" likely to lead to inefficient and inequitable human capital accumulation is in the market for funds. On the principle of acting directly upon the problem at hand, a good argument may therefore be made in favour of state intervention in financing education. But what form should this financial assistance take and on what should it be spent?

In most countries, the direct costs (teachers' salaries, capital costs of facilities, and the costs of materials and supplies) are typically borne entirely by the State, at least at the primary school level. Some school systems charge user fees at the secondary level, and a number of universities and colleges charge some form of tuition. The direct costs of education per pupil broadly rise with the level of education, and are far higher at tertiary level than at secondary school. The indirect costs of earnings foregone are also much greater at tertiary level, for earnings rise both with age and prior education.

What are the merits of offering free or subsidized tuition and of offering stipend grants in lieu of some part of earnings foregone, versus ensuring the availability of loans to cover both? Since tertiary education is by far the most expensive, any grant system is likely to subsidize each student most at the tertiary level. But in virtually all education systems, it is the children of the élite who continue into higher education, even if this education is heavily subsidized. Grants, particularly at the higher education level, then amount to a very substantial transfer payment to the wealthy. This is difficult to justify. Loans offered or ensured by the State can be used to satisfy equal opportunity without an element of subsidy to the rich. Indeed even a progressive element can always be inserted into such a loan system by tying rates of repayment to post-graduation earnings.

On the grounds of promoting greater equality within and across generations a higher rate of subsidy would thus seem warranted for basic education than at the tertiary level. But is this efficient?

State spending on different levels of education

Of course the rate of pass through from primary to secondary to tertiary education may be subject to state control, either through rationing places or through setting minimum examination standards for entry. The manpower implications of this mix amongst primary, secondary and tertiary education and hence of the mix in public spending across these education levels are profound. A manpower planning approach to this decision projects the occupational content of future production, assigns a required level of education to each occupation, and consequently determines the "required" net addition from each level of education over the coming years. As noted already in this paper, such an approach makes some powerful assumptions which may not be met. In practice, the level of education "required" for a specific occupation depends upon the structure of education available in the labour force: taxi drivers with university degrees are not uncommon in some parts of the world. But in addition, even if the assumptions of the manpower planning approach were approximated they would still fail to take account of some potentially important issues already mentioned. In particular the manpower planning approach, as the name implies, focuses (exclusively) upon generating manpower. For many societies this is not the only (or even the major) perceived role for education. Promotion of ethical values, national unity and perhaps a common language, as well as producing responsible citizens, are frequently seen as primary objectives of the educational system, and the manpower planning approach in its basic form takes no account of these.

The chief alternative normally recommended instead of manpower planning is rate-of-return analysis. However, some serious shortcomings must also be recognized with this approach. What are these difficulties?

A first step in calculating the social rate of return to education is to compute the private rate of return. In essence this is taken to be the percentage increase in earnings per year of school. In deriving this percentage increase there are already difficulties. To examine the percentage increment to pay only for those in work misses both the potentially important problem of unemployment among the educated and self-selection among those electing to drop out of the labour force. Whether earnings among the self-employed, both in agriculture and elsewhere, should be treated in common with wage-earnings is also disputed, for self-employment income embodies an element of returns to land and capital. Yet to ignore the self-employed is again to select a special subsample for examination. In principle corrections for all of these sample selection issues may be made, though this does not always occur.

Disentangling the effect of schooling from other influences or earnings is not always easy. Two examples may suffice to illustrate. If individuals who are inherently gifted continue their education longer and one observes the educated with higher pay, is this greater remuneration really a reward to schooling or to the inherent traits? Studies which have included aptitude measures along with amount of schooling in earnings equation estimates have generally found a diminished effect for schooling. But the extent of reduction in the private returns to schooling (and indeed whether there are any returns) is a matter for some dispute. A second illustration stems from the role of age or experience. In calculating the returns to primary education one is comparing the earnings of those dropping out after primary school with those of the completely uneducated. But in most societies today, the only people with no schooling at all are the elderly. Is it true that someone today entering the labour force with no formal schooling could expect the same broad experience as an uneducated person first starting work some decades ago?

If an appropriate measure of the private returns to schooling can be derived, then the next step is to adjust this to calculate the social rate of return. What adjustments need to be made? The most common adjustment is a recognition that in almost all societies private individuals do not bear the full cost of their own education; foregone earnings may be sacrificed by the individual, but fees paid rarely cover the direct costs of education. Other adjustments are far less common, though perhaps no less important. For instance, there is an assumption that higher pay among the educated (and hence higher private returns) reflects higher social product. This may not be true for a number of reasons: the role of public sector pay policy for graduates is central to this, but also such indirect issues as trade protection offered to sectors employing the more highly educated may play an important role in overstating the true returns to education. The social rate of return to schooling ought to be computed in terms of the shadow cost of labour, but this is rarely done. Moreover, few calculations make provision for any of the external benefits from education as outlined in a prior section.

Finally, some limitation must be expressed in applying the social rate of return itself, even if correctly computed. Two aspects at least may be mentioned. The social rate of return at best offers a guide to marginal adjustments. If substantial alterations are made to the educational system, changes in the social rate of return will normally follow. As with any project evaluation methodology this leaves open the possibility that *ex ante* analysis will recommend expansion and *ex post* analysis condemn it. Second, the social rate of return is at best a measure of success of the current schooling system. If the returns to rural primary education appear to be low is this an argument for cutting back on spending on rural primary schools or for investing in improving their quality so that the returns are increased?

If both manpower planning and rate of return analysis are flawed, what guidelines can be offered to public authorities charged with deciding upon spending pattern? There seem to be no simple answers. Perhaps both manpower planning and a rate-of-return analysis may offer some interesting insights, but a rigid application of either would no doubt be a mistake. In the end, no simple summary numbers will suffice, but rather a careful review of the current performance of the educational system must be conducted with a view to discerning spheres for improvement in light of the overall development strategy. This strategy will undoubtedly call for considerable flexibility in today's rapidly changing world. Workers are no longer adhering to one occupation or task for life and hence require adaptability and retraining. A key role for education then resides in providing a basis on which more specific job training and retraining may be founded. In principle, a rate-of-return analysis ought to bring out any merits to basic, rather than occupationally specific training. But this need for flexibility in the workforce is certainly not brought out in any manpower planning exercise, which rather focuses upon the deterministic needs for quite narrow occupational groups.

The curriculum in schools and higher education

In most societies the educational system is perceived as serving multiple roles. Generating a productive workforce may only be one such goal. Other purposes of education may include development of ethical values, establishing a responsible citizenry, or promotion of national unity. This multiplicity of purposes complicates choices with respect to curriculum and fields of study. But even the choice of a curriculum designed to produce a productive workforce is inherently complex.

If flexibility over a lifetime of training and retraining is indeed important, what forms of education best serve as a foundation? Both attitudes to work and cognitive skills matter in determining the efficacy of workers. The basic cognitive skills of numeracy, language ability (and in today's global environment this typically includes English, even for machine operatives in non-English-speaking nations), and increasingly computer skills, seem essential. But rote learning of such skills may be counterproductive in an environment where reasoning capacity matters at all levels. To adapt, adopt and develop new technologies requires reasoning on behalf of the workforce at every stage. Such innovations as quality circles of workers demand feedback from employees on improvements to be introduced in production methods. Workers educated only to execute predefined tasks will offer little in such contexts.

A basic education with an appropriate mix of attitude development and cognitive skill teaching, without stifling creativity and reasoning ability, can serve as a sound basis for more specific training at a later stage. But should this principle of general education be continued at the tertiary level? Is a liberal arts education the ideal in college, rather than pre-professional training? The answer continues to be disputed among educators. But the market does appear to be favouring graduates who have continued into fields more akin to the jobs which they ultimately enter. If the market does a good job of signalling the relative merits of fields, should students be left to choose their own field and the mix adjusted to meet these demands? The costs of providing different lines of education differ quite substantially. Typically students do not cover the full costs even if they pay tuition. Thus the ranking of private returns across different fields of study may be quite different from the ranking of social returns. Private incentives in selecting fields of study cannot then be relied upon entirely. The State may be justified in attempting to influence these choices either by rationing places or by offering differential grants or loans. However, for the State to take such decisions returns us to the difficulty in guessing an appropriate mix of graduates for future development demands. The more general is education, even within higher education, the greater is the flexibility in meeting future market demands. To this extent, the State takes less risk in financing education in general engineering rather than in some narrowly defined form of engineering, leaving specificity to subsequent employers, for instance.

The vocational content of education

A similar argument may be made with respect to vocational education in schools. For the State to select fields of specific vocational education to be taken up in schools is highly risky in terms of future demands. Moreover, to the extent that vocational education detracts from time spent on basic education on which future training may be founded, it may actually be counterproductive.

The efficacy of vocational education continues to be disputed. Certainly a few economies appear to have comparatively successful vocational schooling (such as Germany and Taiwan, China), while in other contexts it has been less useful (as in the United Republic of Tanzania). One generalization which might tentatively be offered is that the more successful vocational schools have actually emphasized the academic portion of the curriculum relatively more and have aimed less at providing highly specific skills at the end of the vocational training.

State involvement in training

So far the discussion in this section has focused exclusively upon formal education. But in many contexts the State is also involved in promoting training. This promotion may take several forms and again a broad distinction may be made between offering financial assistance versus training organized by the public sector.

Financial assistance may be offered either to employers or to individual workers. Grants or tax allowances to employers to compensate for training costs are not uncommon. However, these allowances are more frequently taken up by larger firms, if only because they are better placed to know which allowances exist and because they may find it easier to undertake the necessary administration. The result is then to aid in training employees in large firms who tend to be a fairly privileged group in most developing countries. In particular, loans to employers certainly fail to train the unemployed and even the self-employed. Moreover, spending on in-house training, even within large firms, is difficult for the State to monitor. In consequence, many allowances are confined to off-site training by firms, promoting a bias toward this form of training which may or may not be the more efficient.

Loans, grants and tuition waivers for individuals have the advantage of targeting a wider group. Indeed, such assistance can be targeted at specific groups, such as the poor or those in a declining area, though in principle this might also be feasible through assistance to employers hiring these groups. Perhaps the major disadvantage in offering assistance to individuals rather than employers lies precisely in the fact that many individuals may take up training without a specific job offer, perhaps resulting in a higher redundancy in training.

No matter whether the actual assistance is given to the individual or to an employer, a question arises as to who will provide the training. It is not obvious that the public sector has any innate advantage in organizing training, and in fact private sector training facilities are not uncommon. In the event that such training is organized by the public sector, it may be crucial to involve employers in the decisions with respect to fields of training and even the design of that training. Too often, in the absence of employer involvement, public training programmes offer a mix of fields which fails to match job demands – a product of failed manpower planning either of an explicit or implicit variety. One mechanism which enhances employer involvement is a greater emphasis on apprentice-type training rather than post-school training of persons not yet employed, an emphasis which can be encouraged through financial assistance. However, apprenticeships alone will not suffice, for again these by definition omit those unemployed or not employed by firms large enough to have formal apprentices.

6. Closing remarks

Manpower planning, in the sense of projecting demand for occupations and skills with the intent of matching supply to demand, is founded upon assumptions which strain credibility. Manpower planning, if strictly adhered to, also places exclusive emphasis on the manpower generation role of education.

Yet there are a number of quite legitimate reasons for wanting the State to intervene in the market for education and skills, both on grounds of efficiency and of equality of opportunity. Such interventions require some form of manpower analysis. The major alternative commonly recommended instead of manpower planning is a rate-of-return analysis. But this approach also suffers from a number of inherent difficulties in practice. In the end, government decisions with respect to education and training cannot be guided by any one simple set of numbers. Instead, the management of this system requires constant review to discern areas for improvement. This review must surely involve employers, as well as trainee feedback, if it is to be truly effective.

As the speed of the cycle of product and process innovation accelerates, projecting future comparative advantage and hence skill needs becomes increasingly difficult for the State, for employers and for workers. Employees will need to be trained and retrained as the competitive edge of their country shifts. For this a sound basic education will be required, leaving the specifics of occupational skills for subsequent fine tuning by employers (perhaps aided by state subsidies). To focus on broader skills both serves as an appropriate foundation and removes the need for detailed manpower planning. If temporary bottlenecks do emerge as a result, as the manpower planning model would suggest, these "shortages" can normally be filled through (temporary) immigration if the State is willing to contemplate this route. The alternative is to risk training workers for tasks which they never perform.

4

Planning for vocational education, training and employment: A minimalist approach

Martin Godfrey *[1]

1. Introduction

This paper addresses the question of the scope and content of planning for vocational education, training and employment in developing countries. Its premise is that, since planning uses scarce resources, it should be engaged in as little as is necessary to maximize efficiency and economic growth. The purpose is to define the minimum amount of such planning that is needed and to specify in as much detail as possible the approach that it should take.

2. How much planning is needed?

There is little doubt that a lot of professional energy is expended on planning that is not really necessary. If a certain set of skills can be acquired in a course that lasts only a few months, there is no need to plan intake, enrolment and output for such courses several years ahead. Nor should planners proceed as if government vocational education and training programmes are the only source of such skills, which are acquired also in the home, in enterprises (on and off the job, from employers, from colleagues, from licensors and from suppliers of equipment), and in private training schools (Clark, 1986). Planners should not delude themselves that they have the capacity to plan this wide range of provision in every detail. Nor should they worry about this incapacity; as far as in-service skill development is concerned, demand creates its own supply (Dougherty, 1990).

Recognition of this reality has led some to suggest that training systems could become largely self-regulating, with decisions about content and quantity in the hands of employers, and planners of vocational education and training playing only a facilitating role. This would involve monitoring coordination between employers and training providers, ensuring that the labour market operates efficiently, eliminating distortions affecting decisions about skill acquisition, and promoting the introduction of new skills from abroad (Dougherty, 1986:117).

* Institute of Development Studies, Brighton, Sussex.

[1] Thanks (with the usual disclaimer) are due to A. van Adams for helpful comments; this paper was prepared for the World Bank.

The list of interventions affecting the labour market and the incentive to acquire and impart skills is long. It includes: minimum wage legislation; compression of wage differentials through administered wages in the public sector and high marginal tax rates; schemes of guaranteed employment for graduates; encouragement of capital-intensive methods of production by low or negative real interest rates, protectionist and capital-favouring trade and exchange rate policies and tax regimes; job security regulations; and social insurance charges (World Bank, forthcoming).

Elimination of interventions of this kind is no easy matter. Many of them derive from political objectives, the redefinition of which is beyond the scope of the professional planner. Even if they were swept away at a stroke, it is not clear that training systems could become entirely self-regulating. Market failures[2] are likely to arise because of both positive and negative externalities associated with vocational education and training. On the positive side, anticipation of a skills constraint on growth that would arise if everything was left to individual decisions might reduce inflationary pressures. On the negative side, under certain circumstances, even in an undistorted labour market, market forces alone may induce a level of training that is lower than socially desirable, because of the tendency of firms which do not train to "poach" trained people from firms which do. This possibility arises, for instance, not only because of wage rigidities, but also in extremely low-wage economies, where the normal stratagem of employers faced by potential poachers (shifting the cost of training to employees by paying lower wages to trainees) may have an adverse effect on productivity-through its impact on levels of nutrition (Leibenstein, 1957). In general, also, risk and uncertainty, likely to be accentuated in times of rapid technological change, will be another source of market failure, leading to a less than optimal rate of skill development.

All this means that planners of vocational education and training, even if successful in eliminating interventions, would not be able to leave everything to the market. They would need to design and implement new interventions that would compensate for market failures.[3] These may consist primarily of incentives to employers to increase their provision of in-plant training, but planners would probably also have to live with the continued existence of government vocational/technical schools and training institutions and to advise on the nature of the programmes that they should run. This would involve them not only, in the case of short programmes, in appraisal, monitoring and evaluation through techniques oriented towards the current state of the labour market, but also, in the case of programmes with longer lead times, in looking forward to future directions.

---

[2] Market failure occurs when the free and unimpeded mechanism of market forces does not optimise allocation of resources and maximize national income.

[3] On the more realistic assumption that they would not be completely successful in eliminating distortions, they would need to design and implement "second-best" interventions to compensate for the distortions that remained.

What form should planning not take?

There is no problem in defining the form that such planning should not take – the comprehensive, economy-wide, manpower requirements forecasting approach, which, unhappily, has never been more popular with governments of the developing world.[4] This approach has a limited role, in defining the scale of adjustment that is likely to be needed in the labour market in the face of educational expansion, or in estimating the impact on the numbers joining the labour force of various changes in policy, for instance variations in repetition or dropout rates, in rates of transition from one level of the school system to another and in labour force participation rates (see Godfrey, 1987:7-38 for further discussion). But one thing it cannot be used for is to derive an economy's occupational training needs.

This is only partly because of the weaknesses in the assumptions underlying it, first pointed out by Blaug (1967, 1970) and since re-emphasized in countless economists' critiques: zero substitutability between labour and other factors, between workers of different educational levels within occupations, and between occupations; insensitivity of the fixed coefficients used in the forecasting formula to variations in cost of schooling and training, in wages and in prices of all kinds; and optimality of the coefficients that happen to be observed. Equally important are the practical problems associated with this approach.[5]

The first and most striking of these is the extremely poor quality of the occupational data on which it is based. In the Indonesian 1980 census (the basis of a whole generation of forecasts), for instance, 17 per cent of those enumerated as architects and engineers, 20 per cent of life scientists and related technicians, medical, dental, veterinary and related semiprofessional workers and 64 per cent of physical scientists and related technicians were found to have primary schooling and below!

Even if the data were of perfect quality there would be problems in trying to use them for training needs analysis. They are usually too highly aggregated. The two-digit International Standard Classification of Occupations (ISCO), which is most commonly used, jumbles together a number of occupations of similar level but with different training requirements (e.g. spinners, weavers, knitters, dyers). It also combines different levels, as in the cases of physical scientists and related technicians, etc. Desegregation to the three-digit level (nearly three hundred categories in ISCO) would help but is unlikely to be sufficient, particularly at the professional/technical level; electrical and electronics engineers are still lumped together, for instance, as are biologists and zoologists, and bacteriologists and pharmacologists.

Even if occupational categories were sufficiently desegregated to be homogeneous, categorization by occupation is not coterminous with that by skill level. Statistically generalizable surveys cannot, in their nature, capture the extent to which those classified in a particular occupation (even if accurately so) are able to perform competently. Yet this is the crucial baseline information required from any survey that purports to guide identification of training needs. It would help to know how

[4] Seven out of ten market economies covered by a recent review of Asian experience in human resource planning have used this approach (Amjad, 1987).

[5] See Godfrey (1987) for further discussion.

many in each occupation had appropriate formal qualifications (likely to be a small proportion of the total).[6] But this still leaves out of account those who are adequately skilled though lacking formal training. In the absence of information of this kind, the use of the total number in the occupational category as a base for projecting demand for trained workers in this category would be grossly misleading.

Even if comprehensive information about the current capacities of the work-force were available, to decide whether new training programmes were needed it would be necessary to know all about existing training programmes. As already emphasized, this does not mean only government training programmes, which may indeed represent only a small proportion of total training, in comparison with on-the-job and off-the-job training by companies, private training institutions, licensors, suppliers of equipment, etc. To collect comprehensive and updated information about government training programmes alone would be difficult enough. In Indonesia, for instance, even for the 45 state universities there are no good cohort data. For the Manpower Department's vocational training centres there are figures on targets but not on actual enrolment. For private training institutions it would be more difficult still; even the number of private universities in Indonesia (well over 500) is not exactly known. In the case of company training, training by equipment suppliers, etc., it would be virtually impossible. But if you don't know what you've got how do you know what you need?

Many manpower planners try to evade this issue by simply assuming that supply by educational qualification determines supply by occupation (e.g. see Cohen, 1986; Crouch et al., 1985). In other words an education/occupation matrix is applied, amazingly enough, to the supply as well as to the demand side, as if each school-leaver were labelled to a single occupational destination. This is, of course, no help at all for training needs analysis, since it assumes away the need to think about training provision. And if occupational projections are not for training needs analysis, what are they for?

In the light of the foregoing and of the inherent uncertainty of the future, it is hardly surprising that forecasts based on the manpower requirements approach have turned out to be wildly inaccurate. This has been demonstrated over the years by evaluations of a wide range of forecasts (Hollister, 1967; Jolly and Colclough, 1972; Ahamad and Blaug, 1973; Amjad, 1987).

In short, even if the conceptual objections to the methodology that are usually emphasized are waived, and it is accepted on its own terms, there is simply not enough information to enable manpower projections to be used to derive detailed and precise training needs. It is actually dishonest to pretend otherwise, however much high-level decision-makers may be clamouring for such figures.

It is certainly true that decision-makers at these higher levels still want forecasts – to the exasperation of the critics of this approach. Having demonstrated that "making long-term projections of manpower supply and demand on the basis of general economy-wide methods is not likely to be a very fruitful exercise for a developing country", Hollister (1983:69) has to recognize that, "unfortunately, in many developing countries this is precisely the activity which has taken up most of the time and resources of manpower planning groups". Dougherty (1983:48) glumly concedes that

---

[6] A careful (and time-consuming) investigation in Kenya revealed that only 22 per cent of those in engineering technician occupations in 1979 had formal technician qualifications (Bennell, 1980).

"the view that planning consists of the preparation of detailed forecasts of supply and demand may be deeply entrenched even where the approach is patently impracticable". Amjad (1985) observes that precise quantitative projections "have little bearing on actual policy implementation but the demand to generate them has in no way decreased over the years". Indeed their popularity may even have increased since the early 1970s: "the critical bombardment appears to have had no effect on practitioners' use of the approach and more and more countries have in fact adopted it", even though "individuals in manpower development units are sometimes almost apologetic about their forecasting work" (Psacharopoulos and Hinchliffe, 1983:12). Ironically the World Bank may have helped to encourage the survival of the methodology since, at least until a recent change of heart, "most requests for educational loans from the World Bank and most project appraisals" have been "justified on the grounds of manpower requirements" (Psacharopoulos and Woodhall, 1985:77).

What form should planning take ?

The fact that manpower projections cannot be used to derive detailed and precise training needs is nothing for planners of vocational education and training to worry about. Detailed forecasts are not needed. What is needed, by students, their parents, teachers, trainers, jobseekers, employees and employers, is reliable and timely information about the state of the various labour markets for qualified people and a structure of incentives that will reward both those who acquire and those who impart skills. Meeting these information needs will be one of the main functions of planners in this field.

The rest of the work of such planners will be concerned with designing and implementing new interventions and in monitoring and evaluating existing programmes. Five stages can be distinguished in this process:

(a) They will identify problems. For instance, it may be that graduates from government technical training centres are no more successful in obtaining jobs in industry than are those with a similar level of education but without such training, and that the centres have chronic financial problems.

(b) They will analyse the causes of these problems. In this example they may note that employers are involved neither in the design and finance of the technical training centre's programmes nor in the selection of trainees.

(c) They will appraise options for the solution of the problems. For example, in this case, such options might include: (i) closing down the centres; (ii) simple privatization of the centres, with unsubsidized fees paid by employers or trainees; (iii) their operation within the framework of a levy-grant system (whereby all firms above a certain size are levied or taxed and those which train are reimbursed by a grant); (iv) their operation within a system of tax allowances for firms' training expenses; or (iv) an entirely new type of government training centre, subsidized as before but with close links with industry. Faced with such a range of options, planners will try to predict their outcomes and costs and compare them, to determine which promises to be the best course of action.

(d) They will monitor the implementation of whichever solutions to problems are chosen. Monitoring a project, at a midterm stage, will be concerned with ways of improving it (by redesigning its mode, curricula, management, etc.) or perhaps with decisions about its continuation, expansion or replication.

(e) Finally, they will from time to time evaluate the various programmes of vocational education and training in which the government is involved. Such evaluation comes at the end of a project or programme phase and is mainly concerned with learning lessons for designing subsequent projects.

The crucial distinction in such planning is between programmes for which the time between decision-making and labour market outcome is relatively short (say, two years or less) and programmes for which this lead time is long. The classic example of the first type of programme is the courses of six months or less, for mechanics, welders, carpenters, bricklayers, electricians, etc., run by many government training centres. At the other extreme are specialist university degree courses, often involving postgraduate training, for which the lead time may be a decade or more.

Procedures to be followed in the first two stages of planning – identification of problems and analysis of causes – will not differ much between short and long programmes. Essentially the aim in both cases will be to find out what is going on, both inside the training institutions and in the relevant labour markets. This may involve some formal, statistically generalizable, baseline studies but, initially at least, will be more a matter of talking informally to employers, trade unionists, researchers, journalists, educators, trainers and government officials about processes and problems in vocational education and training and in labour markets.

At these stages, also, it may be useful to assemble and analyse some simple indicators of the labour market situation. For instance, information may be available about the number of unfilled vacancies currently being advertized by employers for the relevant occupational category. However, data on vacancies need to be treated with care. Vacancies are often filled internally, rather than being advertised or reported to employment exchanges. Particularly within the public sector, the number of "vacancies" reported to interviewers or in questionnaires often represents the posts it would be desirable to fill if finance were available, rather than posts for which active recruitment (backed by the power to pay) is in process. Also, of course, the number of vacancies at a given moment (a stock) may be a misleading indicator of the flow of future demand over time.

It is a common practice to combine information about vacancies with information about unemployment of people in the same occupational category. Thus if the unemployed/vacancies ratio is found to be equal to one this part of the labour market is judged to be in balance; if the ratio is below one (i.e. the number of vacancies exceeds the number of unemployed) this is taken to suggest that there is a need to expand training provision. However, even in industrialized countries with highly developed social security and employment exchange systems the unemployed/vacancies ratio has not been found to be a reliable indicator. In countries where few people use the official employment exchanges, and where many of those who do are not unemployed but looking for something better, this ratio is likely to be even less helpful.

The number of expatriates employed in the relevant job category may be a more useful indicator of excess demand. An indicator of the need for local training facilities, also, may be the number of students going abroad for training of this kind. And, where local training facilities are available, an indicator of a need for further provision is the number of applications in relation to the number of places; the higher the ratio of applicants to places, the higher the probable payoff to graduates of this type of training. Finally, the planners may look at the impact of earnings over time of the type of training in question. If relative earnings of this occupation vis-à-vis similar occupations are rising, this may signal an emerging shortage.

While the procedures to be followed in the first two stages will, thus, differ little between long and short programmes, the content of the final three stages – appraisal, monitoring and evaluation – will vary with the length of lead time between decision and output. For this reason, in the discussion of these stages of planning that follows, short and long programmes are treated separately.

Planning for programmes with short lead times

To some extent the planning of short programmes can be handed over to those who run them. This involves making training institutions more flexible and more responsive to the changing situation in local labour markets by devolving decision-making and financial responsibility to managers of such institutions and involving local employers in their design, management and finance. This alone should ensure that training programmes are relevant to the current needs of the local economy, but occasional appraisal, monitoring and evaluation through cost/outcome analysis may also be useful. For such analysis planners ideally need to know the outcome of the route to skill acquisition that is under consideration (in terms of its impact on skill and on performance in the labour market) and how much it costs (from the point of view of society as a whole, of government and of the individual). Broadly the same method will be used in appraisal, monitoring and evaluation, but the data on cost and outcome used in an appraisal will inevitably be more speculative.

The various passible routes to technical/vocational skill acquisition are summarized in figure 4.1. A school-leaver (from a general or a technical/vocational school) may go straight into employment without further training and may acquire the skills needed entirely from learning by doing. Alternatively he/she may undergo purposive training, either in-plant (on the job or off the job) or outside the plant (part time or full time). Or some combination of any or all of these modes may be used. Some examples of possible combinations are given in figure 4.1.

The question of interest to planners is: how do routes to skill acquisition which include specific, short, government programmes compare (in cost/outcome terms) with those that do not or with those that do to a lesser extent? The question is relevant for any level/type of training (professional, managerial, semi-professional, skilled, semi-skilled) and any sector.[7]

---

[7] See Hunting et al. (1986: chapter 3) for a detailed, general description of the approach to answering this question.

In the case of skilled-level technical/vocational training for larger wage-employing firms in non-agricultural sectors, for instance, the question could be approached by selecting four samples of comparable school-leavers: (1) secondary technical school-leavers who have attended government technical training centres; (2) secondary technical school-leavers who have undergone only in-plant on-the-job training (route 3.A.(i) in figure 4.1) ; (3) general secondary school-leavers who have attended government technical training centres; (4) general secondary school-leavers who have undergone only in-plant on-the-job training.

On the cost side, the task would be to establish the cost of the post-school component in each of the four routes. Information on both capital and current cost would be needed, though which costs could be treated as variable would depend on the question under consideration. In particular, is it a decision merely about expanding or reducing enrolment or does it involve building new institutions? A large part of the cost of on the-job training would be the reduction in output resulting from employing a trainee and using supervisors' time for training.

On the outcome side, two types of outcome could be looked at. Skill outcome could be measured, for the two samples that attended technical training centres, at the end of their period of training or in the early stages of their first job. The point would be to measure the extent to which secondary technical and secondary general school graduates still differ in their levels of job-related skill after having completed training in the centres. Special tests would probably have to be administered for this purpose. Further tests could be given to all four sample groups after they have worked for about a year. To what extent do the skill levels of graduates of training centres differ from those of purely on-the-job trainees, and in each case what difference does type of secondary schooling make?

As far as labour market outcome is concerned, two types of study would be needed. One would compare earnings and employment experience of secondary technical and secondary general school graduates who (a) have and (b) have not attended training centres. The second would look at the relative progress through larger firms of those employees who have only had in-plant training and those who have had out-of-plant training, again distinguishing between secondary technical and secondary general school graduates.

Various comparisons of cost and outcome would now be needed. At the simplest level these would include accurate estimates of unit cost (current and capital social cost, cost to government and private cost) of each of the types of training under consideration. As far as skill development is concerned, cost effectiveness comparisons could be made. Which is the most cost-effective route to the acquisition of industrial skills: secondary general + training centre, secondary technical + training centre, secondary general + on-the-job training, secondary technical + on-the-job training, etc.? The criterion would be cost per unit of skill improvement. Finally, and most ambitiously, cost-benefit estimates could be made of these various routes in the usual way, whether in the form of benefit/cost ratio, net present value or internal rate of return.

Such techniques, based on the current state of the labour market, would suffice for appraising, monitoring or evaluating short training programmes, the design of which could be changed fairly quickly. For programmes with long lead times, how-

Figure 4.1. Routes to technical or vocational skill acquisition

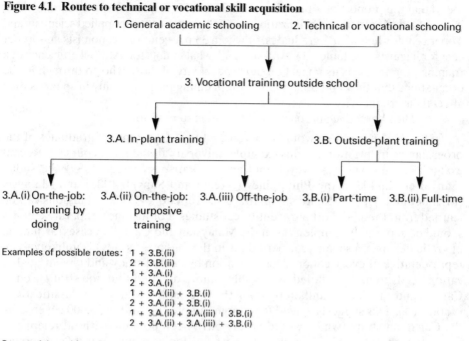

Examples of possible routes: 1 + 3.B.(ii)
2 + 3.B.(ii)
1 + 3.A.(i)
2 + 3.A.(i)
1 + 3.A.(ii) + 3.B.(i)
2 + 3.A.(ii) + 3.B.(i)
1 + 3.A.(ii) + 3.A.(iii) ı 3.B.(i)
2 + 3.A.(ii) + 3.A.(iii) + 3.B.(i)

Source: Adapted from Blaug, 1981.

ever, cost/outcome analysis alone may be a misleading guide for planners' decisions. Structural changes in the economy may alter the social profitability of long courses by the time their graduates emerge. An alternative approach to the analysis of future directions needs to be devised, combining (a) current rate-of-return analysis and (b) analysis of expected structural change in the economy. This is the task to which we turn in the next section.

Planning for programmes with long lead times

The focus of this alternative approach to analysis of future directions for government vocational education and training programmes with long lead times would be not on occupation but on type of educational or training qualification. This is partly because (as already discussed above), of all the statistics handled by labour economists, those concerning occupation are of the poorest quality. It could also be argued that technological change is undermining the very concept of occupation. In Japan there is already "not such a fixed distinction between the roles of workers... We can distinguish roles, if we want to. But it is very hard to grasp the real situation, because enterprises often alter the allotment of roles among their employees whenever the need arises" (ILO/APSDEP, 1988:143). In any case correspondence between academic specialization and eventual occupation is far from complete. A 1981 study of higher education and the labour market in the Philippines, for instance, found that the proportion of employed graduates of the previous two years working in their field of academic specialization was only 73 per cent for applied scientists and 47 per cent for liberal arts graduates, of whom 33 per cent for economists and 17 per cent for linguists (see table 4.1). And, after all, what counts for external efficiency of a training programme is its impact on the productivity of those who go through it; the occupations that they end up in matter, for planning purposes, only in so far as they affect their productivity.

The alternative approach would have six steps as follows:

(a) The first step would be a tracer study of a sample of graduates of the programmes in question (in this example university first degree courses). Recent examples of this type of survey, from Canada (Statistics Canada, 1989), the Sudan (Sanyal et al., 1987), the Philippines (Arcelo and Sanyal, 1987) and Malaysia (Mehmet and Yip, 1986) are summarized in Appendix A. Useful lessons can be learned from these and other recent tracer studies. For instance, separate cohorts should be separately sampled (as in the Malaysian and Canadian cases); a jumble of graduates over a seven-year period (as in the Sudanese study) is unlikely to be representative of every cohort. Desegregation by field of study and type of qualification needs to be as detailed as possible – more detailed than the strata used in Canada and the Sudan, and more along the lines of the Malaysian classifications (Table A.1). This suggests a need for a large sample – if not the 36,000 covered by the Canadian study (which would hardly have been possible without telephone interviews, an unfeasible technology in most developing countries), at least enough to ensure analysable numbers by detailed field of study. It is also important to achieve a high response rate (as in the Canadian and Malaysian surveys); if response is as low as in the Philippines, 49 per cent, there is a high risk that respondents are unrepresentative. In countries such as Indonesia, where there are important qualitative differences between universities of different types, outcomes could usefully be desegregated not only by sex, field of study and qualification, but also by type of university (distinguishing for instance between top and other, public and private universities).

However, questionnaires do not need to be as long, for our limited purpose, as in the studies reviewed in Appendix A. In particular, we are interested not in graduates' opinions, attitudes, motives, job satisfaction, etc., but only in what has happened to them.[8] A streamlined version of the Malaysian questionnaire, as in Appendix B, which manages to obtain most of the information needed about personal and family characteristics and labour market experience from 18 questions, would probably suffice.

(b) Analysis of the cost of the courses would be the next step. Questions 9 to 12 in our streamlined Malaysian questionnaire (Appendix B) show how information about private cost might be obtained from graduates. The Malaysian study also assembled the kind of data on the expenditure of universities that would be needed for social cost calculations (Mehmet and Yip: chapter IV). Recurrent and capital

---

[8] Including their remuneration. It is extraordinary to find a tracer study such as that carried out in the Sudan (Sanyal et al., 1987) which did not think it worthwhile asking a question about remuneration.

Table 4.1. The Philippines, academic qualifications compared with jobs obtained by 1979-81 university graduates, 1981

Field of study	% of graduates employed in the field of specialization
Liberal arts programmes	
Economics	33
Humanities	33
Languages	17
Mass communications	57
Mathematics	56
Music and fine arts	82
Physical sciences	50
Social sciences	47
Average	47
Applied sciences	
Agriculture	71
Business administration	92
Dentistry	100
Education	60
Engineering	76
Fisheries	67
Foreign service	40
Home economics	42
Law	87
Medicine	96
Medical technology	80
Nautical science	67
Nutrition	58
Vocational-technical	62
Average	73

Source: Arcelo and Sanyal, 1987, Table 4.19.

development expenditure, deflated by the consumer price index, are analysed by university and by the eight broad groups of study fields shown in Table A.1. For our purposes, desegregation of cost would need to go further, to the same level of detail as that used in the tracer study; this may imply a need to collect cost data direct from universities, rather than from centralized data sources.

(c) The results of the tracer study and the cost estimates could then be embodied in calculations of the internal rate of return (private and social) on each type of course in the usual way. The studies of the Philippines and Malaysia summarized in Appendix A exemplify different ways of approaching this. In the case of the Philippines a well-known short-cut formula was used to compute private rate of return only.[9] The Malaysian study used the full formulae for both private and social rates of return, making explicit assumptions about the length of working life of university and high school graduates, rates of salary increment,[10] rates of price inflation, marginal tax rates and the proportion of additional lifetime earnings attributable to university education. Rates of return were calculated not only by broad field of study, but also by ethnic group and for scholars and non-scholars. Given further desegregation along the lines already discussed, it forms a useful model for this part of our alternative approach.

(d) The fourth step would be to build up as detailed a picture as possible of likely structural changes in the economy over the planning period. The particular aim would be to identify sectors and branches which are likely to decline relatively, in employment terms, and those which are likely to increase in relative importance (including branches which do not at present exist in the economy in any substantial way).

For example, Table 4.2 shows some targets set for selected industrial branches and for other broad sectors in Malaysia as part of a recent medium- and long-term industrial master plan (Malaysian Industrial Development Authority 1985), based on estimates of the likely impact of technological change on productivity and competitiveness.

As can be seen, the expectation in this particular case is of above-average growth in employment in chemical and plastic products, machinery and engineering, and electrical and electronics, and of a decline in food and beverages and textiles and apparel. Employment in manufacturing as a whole is expected to grow more slowly than in other sectors, with construction, electricity, gas and water, and transport, storage and communications showing the highest growth rates, and agriculture and mining and quarrying the lowest.

This kind of forecasting is already common as part of the planning process in many developing countries, so the extra work involved would not be arduous, although the time period would need to be longer than the usual five-year plan, and it would need to be based on a realistic assessment of the dynamic comparative advantage of the economy.

(e) Fifthly, a comprehensive survey of employment of graduates of the courses under review would be mounted. The data to be collected from each of the sectors/branches surveyed would include the detailed educational qualification, by field of study, level and institution, of each graduate employee, and the number of such employees as a proportion of total employment in that branch.

---

[9] The formula, from Psacharopoulos and Sanyal (1981) is:

$$r = \frac{Y - Yfor}{5\,(Yfor + C)}$$

where Y is initial income, Yfor is foregone income, C is the private direct cost, and 5 is the assumed length of college studies.

[10] The authors' task in this respect was made easier by the fact that 85 per cent of their employed respondents were working in the public sector, although it casts some doubt on the value for policy of their social rate-of-return calculations!

Table 4.2. Malaysia, targets for employment growth rates by industrial branch and other sectors, 1985-95

Industrial branch	Empl. in 1985 ('000)	Target rate (% per annum)	Other sectors	Empl. in 1985 ('000)	Target rate (% per annum)
Food & beverages	88	-0.8	Agriculture	1 808	0.6
Textiles & apparel	80	-1.5	Mining & quarrying	57	-0.6
Wood & wood products	80	-0.01	Construction	12	6.9
Chemical & plastic products	24	5.1	Electricity, gas & water	273	6.4
Rubber products	16	3.0	Transport, storage, communications	808	7.9
Non-metallic mineral products	26	-0.5	Wholesale, etc.	184	4.5
Ferrous metal	15	3.3	Finance, etc.	100	3.5
Non-ferrous metal	2	-3.3	Government	1 359	1.7
Machinery & engineering	43	4.7	**Total all sectors**	**5 208**	**3.0**
Electrical & electronics	107	2.8			
Transport equipment	20	1.5			
Total manufacturing	**501**	**1.5**			

Source: Malaysian Industrial Development Authority (1985: Table III-1).

A partial model for this step in the alternative approach is provided by the survey of graduates of universities and post-secondary education carried out in Israel after each of its population censuses, most recently in 1984 (Israel, Central Bureau of Statistics, 1987). This survey is much more detailed than is necessary for our purpose (the questionnaire has 28 pages and 90 questions!) and is administered directly to individual graduates (a sample of 10,000 graduates in 1984, with a 91 per cent response rate) rather than through their employers or workplaces. But some of the information obtained corresponds exactly to that required here. Educational details asked for include the name of the academic degree or diploma, the field of study (with 97 fields coded) and the name of the academic institution (whether at home or abroad). The questions asked about employment include one about "the main activity of your place of work". This allows tabulation by level of degree, field of study and economic branch, as shown in Table 4.3. A much more detailed desegregation of economic branches would be possible; other tables show as many as thirty sectors and subsectors.

In the case of the government services sector, often the predominant employer of university graduates, the information required could usually be obtained directly from personnel records, without the need for a questionnaire survey.

In the case of sectors and branches which do not yet exist in the country in any substantial way or in which rapid technological change is in prospect, it would be useful to collect data, at a similar level of detail, from another economy at a more advanced level of development. The idea here would not be to use the pattern of employment in the higher-income economy as a "target" for the lower-income economy in such sectors and branches. This would be misleading since the optimum

Table 4.3. Israel, employed university graduates, by field of study and economic branch, 1984 (thousands)

Field of study	Industry	Financing & business services	Public & community services	Other	Total
First degree[1] – Grand total	17.0	23.7	50.6	17.9	109.3
General humanities	0.5	0.8	7.2	1.6	10.1
Languages, literature, religion	0.5	0.8	7.5	1.4	10.2
Education & teacher training	0.2	0.2	4.6	0.6	2.7
Fine & applied arts	0.5	0.3	1.9	1.0	3.7
Social sciences/ business/administration	4.8	9.1	12.9	5.8	32.6
Medicine & paramedical studies	0.3	–	2.7	1.3	4.3
Mathematics/ statistics/computers	1.0	1.1	2.3	0.5	5.0
Physical sciences	0.5	0.4	1.3	0.5	2.6
Biological sciences	0.3	0.1	3.0	0.4	3.8
Agriculture	0.2	0.1	1.2	1.1	2.5
Architecture	0.1	1.5	0.2	0.3	2.2
Construction/ civil engineering	0.2	1.7	0.4	1.1	3.4
Electrical/electronic/ computer engineering	2.8	0.7	1.3	0.5	5.2
Mechanical engineering	2.3	0.7	0.9	0.5	4.4
Chemical/metallurgical/ material/extraction engineering	0.8	0.1	0.3	0.1	1.2
Industrial & management engineering	1.1	0.5	0.3	0.4	2.4
Other engineering	0.7	0.2	0.4	0.1	1.4

– = nil or negligible.   [1] Similar breakdowns are made of second and third degree holders.

Source: Israel, Central Bureau of Statistics, 1988.

degree of "graduate-intensiveness" in any sector and any country will depend on, among other things, salary levels and differentials in that country. Thus data would need to be collected on graduate employment not only in the "new" sector or branch in the comparator country but also in some of the older industries in that country, with a view to assessing the relative graduate-intensity of the sector/branch in question and the difference in its pattern of graduate employment.

For example, the medium- and long-term industrial master plan for Malaysia, already discussed above, compared the proportion of engineers and technicians in the workforce of various industrial branches in Malaysia in 1981 with that in a number of more advanced economies ten years earlier. Table 4.4 summarizes these data, taken from Zymelman (1984).

They are not ideal for our purpose, since they are based on occupational definitions rather than qualifications; desegregation by field of study and branch could usefully be more detailed; and, in a world of rapidly changing technology, a comparison with, say, the Singapore or the Republic of Korea of today would be more useful than one with the United States. or the United Kingdom of ten years

Table 4.4. Engineers and technicians by industrial branch as a share of the labour force in selected countries, 1970 (percentages)

Industrial branch	United States	United Kingdom	Germany, Fed. Rep. of	Sweden	Singapore	Malaysia[1]
Food & beverages	2.2	1.7	1.3	3.4	1.5	1.4
Textiles & apparel	1.4	0.9	2.0	2.2	0.5	0.6
Wood & wood products	1.4	0.9	n.a.	n.a.	0.3	0.3
Chemical & plastic products	13.4	8.6	13.2	16.3	4.0	3.4
Rubber products	4.9	3.3	5.0	6.4	1.1	1.7
Non-metallic mineral products	4.1	3.0	3.9	6.6	1.9	1.1
Ferrous metal	4.1	4.6	n.a.	n.a.	2.7	2.2
Non-ferrous metal	5.3	4.5	n.a.	n.a.	2.2	2.5
Machinery & engineering	7.7	10.6	11.1	12.7	5.7	2.5
Electrical & electronics	14.2	11.4	12.2	18.5	5.2	5.1
Transport equipment	10.0	7.6	8.4	12.3	3.5	10.0
Total manufacturing sector	6.1	5.5	6.5	8.4	2.3	2.4

n.a. = not available.   [1] Figures for 1981.

Source: Malaysian Industrial Development Authority (1985).

earlier. They were, also, used in a mechanical way by the authors of the Malaysian plan to set targets for Malaysian manufacturing industry (8 per cent of the overall workforce to be engineers and technicians by 1995, with a range between 2 and 15 per cent for individual branches). Nevertheless, if we treat the data as if they were qualification-based and ignore the overaggregation, they can illustrate what would be involved in an alternative cross-country comparison.

Thus the point to note from Table 4.4 is not the precise value of the percentages in each branch in each of the more industrialized countries, but the relative engineer-intensity of each branch. If, for instance, the United Kingdom were taken as a model, the figures do not imply a need to raise the proportion of engineer/technicians in the workforce of, say, the electrical and electronics industry to 11.4 per cent in order to achieve British levels of productivity in that branch (which would be the old manpower forecasting assumption). What they do suggest is that the electrical/electronics industry is a relatively engineer-intensive branch. In all the countries in the table the proportion of engineers/technicians in that branch is double or more than double the average for manufacturing industry as a whole. This is what would have to be taken into account in thinking about the implications of establishing or expanding the electrical/electronics industry.

(f) Finally, the data collected on expected structural change in the economy would be used to estimate what is likely to happen to rates of return on each specialization.

In the case of demand for graduates in the government services sector a detailed projection of demand should be possible. In many cases (e.g. teachers, doctors, nurses, police) a first set of targets by occupation could be related to demographic, social or political norms. However, actual demand will be constrained by revenue possibilities (and it is demand rather than targets which is of interest here), so projections of government revenue and recurrent expenditure would form the framework for this exercise. Moreover, figures on demand by occupational category would have to be translated into demand by academic specialization (reflecting desired increases in hiring standards) before conclusions could be drawn about the likely impact on patterns of rates of return of changes in the government services sector.

For example, in the Malaysia of 1985, given the commitment to a freeze on public sector recruitment, the expectation would have been of only a modest growth of government recurrent expenditure on personal emoluments over the next ten years or so, though with some substitution of senior for junior posts and some increase in the average educational level of civil servants.[11] Given the need for staffing levels in social services such as health, education and police to rise roughly in line with population (and for salary levels in these services to be high enough to continue to attract people into these professions), the amount left over for salaries in other government services would have been expected to be severely constrained. The negative impact of all this on the demand for graduates in these services (the pattern of whose academic specializations would be known from personnel records) would be offset by the educational upgrading process, but the rate of growth in such demand, assuming no fall in the real value of salaries, would have been expected to be below historical levels.

In the rest of the economy the main focus of interest would be on the more volatile and graduate-intensive sectors. Data collected on these and other sectors would enable a judgement to be reached about the direction of the likely net effect of structural change on rates of return by academic specialization.

For instance, in the case of the manufacturing sector, the Malaysian planners combined their assumptions about growth in employment by branch (Table 4.2) with those about engineer-intensity (based on the international comparisons in Table 4.4) to yield forecasts of the number of engineers per branch by 1995. If these are scaled down somewhat to allow for differences in the factor markets of the various countries in Table 4.4, they can be used for illustrative purposes. Thus Table 4.5 shows forecasts of stocks of engineers in the selected branches, on the assumption that graduate-intensities will be only 75 per cent of those predicted in the Industrial Master Plan.

As can be seen the fastest rate of growth in employment of engineers and technicians is expected in the wood and wood products and chemical and plastics products industries, but by far the largest absolute increase, reflecting both overall expansion and a more than doubling of engineer intensity, is expected in the electrical and electronics industry.

The next task is to translate these forecasts for engineers and technicians as a whole into forecasts by fields of study. Table 4.6 shows the assumptions made for this purpose (based on expectations about the impact of technological change) about patterns of specialization in the branches of industry covered by the industrial master plan.

---

[11] This is reflected in the forecast of the industrial master planners (Malaysian Industrial Development Authority, 1985) that total employment in the government sector would grow at an annual average rate of only 1.7 per cent between 1985 and 1995 (see Table 4.2).

Table 4.5. Malaysia, derivation of the forecast of the number of engineers and technicians employed in selected industrial branches, 1995, and rates of change, 1985-95

Industrial branch	Total empl. ('000)		Eng/tech. (% of total)		Eng/tech. ('000)		Rate of change (% per annum)
	1985	1995	1985	1995	1985	1995	1985-95
Food & beverages	87	81	1.4	2.4	1.2	1.9	4.6
Textiles & apparel	80	67	0.6	1.7	0.5	1.2	9.3
Wood & wood products	80	70	0.3	2.5	0.2	1.7	21.8
Chemical & plastic products	24	40	3.4	11.0	0.8	4.4	18.1
Rubber products	16	22	1.7	4.7	0.3	1.0	14.1
Non-metallic mineral products	26	25	1.1	4.9	0.3	1.2	15.6
Ferrous metal	15	21	2.2	4.2	0.3	0.9	10.3
Non-ferrous metal	2	1	2.5	5.2	0.1	0.1	4.6
Machinery & engineering	43	68	2.5	6.6	1.1	4.5	15.3
Electrical & electronics	107	141	5.1	11.5	5.5	16.3	11.6
Transport equipment	20	23	10.0	9.5	2.0	2.2	1.0
Total manufacturing sector	501	562	2.4	6.3	12.3	35.4	11.2

Source: Malaysian Industrial Development Authority, 1985.

As can be seen, it is assumed that the distribution within each branch will change little, except for some increase in the share of electrical and electronic engineers and of industrial efficiency engineers at the expense of architects/town planners and civil engineers. Table 4.7 shows, in the first two columns, the forecasts for these manufacturing branches, derived from these coefficients, and for other broad sectors of the economy derived in similar ways.[12]

The fastest rate of growth is expected in the case of industrial efficiency engineering and the slowest in the case of architecture and town planning. Demand for all other specializations is expected to grow at around the same rate. A comparison of the forecasts with earlier experience is only possible in the case of the manufacturing branches covered by the industrial master plan; the only specializations for which demand in these branches is expected to increase at a faster annual rate in 1985-95 than it did in 1980-85 are electrical/electronic and industrial efficiency engineering.

The end-product of all this would be a table showing the best estimate of the current rate of return (social and private) on each qualification, the direction of change in that rate that would be expected over the planning period if the rate at which the stock were growing remained unchanged, and the reasons for that expectation. Table 4.8 shows what this would look like in our Malaysian exercise.

In this case there is one obvious candidate for expansion – industrial efficiency engineering, which combines a high current social rate of return with

---

[12] In a real, rather than illustrative, attempt at the alternative approach, the coefficients would be derived from the survey of graduates described above.

Table 4.6. Malaysia, engineers by field of study, selected industrial branches, 1985 (actual) and 1995 (est.) (per cent)

Specialization	Food & beverages		Textiles/apparel		Wood & products		Chemicals & plastics		Rubber products		Non-metal minerals	
	1985	1995	1985	1995	1985	1995	1985	1995	1985	1995	1985	1995
Urban planning	3	2	3	3	2	–	1	1	–	–	–	–
Civil	9	5	6	2	13	11	7	7	11	6	14	14
Electrical	3	7	5	11	2	8	5	8	2	7	6	6
Mechanical	33	32	52	50	33	30	23	24	30	30	36	36
Chemical	11	11	6	6	2	1	32	32	4	4	15	15
Metallurgy	–	–	–	–	–	–	–	–	–	–	–	–
Mining	6	7	–	–	–	–	2	2	–	–	1	1
Industrial efficiency	17	17	16	15	8	13	4	4	23	23	10	10
Other	28	28	13	14	41	36	26	23	31	31	19	19
Total	100	100	100	100	100	100	100	100	100	100	100	100

Specialization	Ferrous metal		Non-ferrous metal		Machinery & engineering		Electrical/ electronic		Transport equipment	
	1985	1995	1985	1995	1985	1995	1985	1995	1985	1995
Urban planning	–	–	–	–	9	2	–	–	1	1
Civil	9	9	13	4	13	9	6	6	6	6
Electrical	5	5	–	9	11	16	73	73	6	6
Mechanical	30	30	37	37	49	49	8	8	75	75
Chemical	1	1	–	–	1	1	1	1	–	–
Metallurgy	6	6	13	13	2	2	–	–	–	–
Mining	1	1	13	3	1	1	–	–	–	–
Industrial efficiency	26	26	25	25	4	15	5	5	2	2
Other	21	21	–	–	9	6	7	7	10	10
Total	100	100	100	100	100	100	100	100	100	100

– = nil or negligible.

Source: Malaysian Industrial Development Authority, 1985.

prospects of an increase; a case could also be made for electrical/electronic engineering, with a current rate of return around the average but good prospects; architecture and town planning, with a low current rate of return and poor prospects, looks as if it may need cutting back.

Private rates of return are included in the table because they draw attention to the impact of subsidies (which need to be kept under review) and enable planners to monitor the incentives for individuals to enter some professions and avoid others (particularly important for public-sector salaries policy).

An attempt to anticipate some conceptual objections

Alert readers will have detected a family resemblance between the methodology underlying tables 4.5 to 4.8 and the manpower requirements forecasting approach criticized earlier. This cannot be denied in principle, but the role that forecasting plays in our alternative approach is entirely different, in the following respects:

(a) The central focus of the alternative approach is on the rate of return. Forecasting is only used to help estimate whether there will be upward or downward pressures on this rate in each case: it is not used to set targets for enrolment and output for the various specializations; it is merely the translation into (misleadingly precise) figures of tendencies arising from changes in technology and in international markets, so that they can be taken into account in a qualitative way.[13]

(b) The forecasts do not cover all types and levels of skill, but are confined to a few categories for which training needs to be planned well in advance – in our exercise, for instance, the engineering profession. They do need to be economy-wide, however, if all the prospective pressures on rates of return are to be taken into account.

(c) The forecasts concern academic specializations, not occupations.

(d) These specializations are disaggregated into homogeneous categories, corresponding to the courses and qualifications under review.

(e) Since there is no attempt to forecast "surpluses" or "shortages", comprehensive knowledge of existing training provision is not required.

Thus the objectives of forecasting in this alternative approach are much more modest and realistic than in projections of manpower requirements and supply.

Other readers may be more worried about the emphasis placed on rates of return. Familiar conceptual problems certainly arise in the use of earnings as a measure of benefit in calculations of social rate of return.[14] This practice is, of course,

---

[13] The fact that, in the real world, the relationship between rates of return and changes in demand and supply will be iterative is recognized, but the information to model that relationship is never likely to be available. This approach might be regarded as a back-of-envelope substitute for a general equilibrium model of the market for educated labour.

[14] No such problems arise in the use of earnings as a measure of benefit in calculations of private rate of return.

Table 4.7. Malaysia, engineers by field of study and broad sector, 1985 (actual) and 1995 (est.)

Field of study	Manufacturing		Finance, etc.		Public services		Other		All sectors		1985-95	Rate of growth
	1985	1995	1985	1995	1985	1995	1985	1995	1985	1995	Increase	(%)
Urban planning	52	45	669	888	2 041	2 254	428	646	3 189	3 833	+644	1.9
Civil	309	756	892	1 183	4 898	5 410	2 851	4 308	8 950	11 657	+2 707	2.7
Electrical	931	2 994	334	444	10 613	11 722	1 568	2 369	13 446	17 529	+4 083	2.7
Mechanical	1 473	3 296	372	493	6 939	7 664	998	1 508	9 782	12 961	+3 180	2.9
Chemical/ metallurgy/ mining	261	945	74	99	2 857	3 156	143	215	3 335	4 415	+1 079	2.8
Industrial efficiency	325	1 040	186	247	1 633	1 803	713	1 077	2 856	4 167	+1 311	3.8
Other engineering	624	1 710	111	148	4 082	4 508	428	646	5 254	7 012	+1 767	2.9
Total	3 975	10 785	2 638	3 501	33 064	36 518	7 127	10 770	43 803	61 574	+14 771	2.8

Source: Malaysian Industrial Development Authority, 1985.

Table 4.8. Format for planning for vocational education and training programmes with long lead times: Engineers in Malaysia

Programme	Rates of return 1985 (%)		Expected direction of change 1985-95	Reasons for expectation
	Private	Social		
Architecture/ town planning	9.4	6.0	Down	Reduction in intensity leading to fall in manufacturing; weak rise in other sectors; deceleration
Civil engineering	12.4	7.9	No change or down	Reduction in intensity in manufacturing leading to below-average growth; deceleration
Electronic engineering	13.1	8.3	Up	Growth of electronics branch and increase in intensity in other sectors; acceleration
Mechanical engineering	15.5	9.9	No change or down	No change in intensity; growth at average rate; deceleration
Chemical/metallurgy/ mining	13.2	8.4	No change	No change in intensity; fast growth of chemical products offset by fall in mining
Industrial efficiency	17.4	11.1	Up	Increase in intensity leading to above average growth; slight acceleration
Other engineering	13.5	8.6	No change	Average growth; slight deceleration
Total	13.5	8.6		

Note: Average rates of return for engineers are those for 1983 graduates from Mehmet and Yip (1986: Tables 5-1 and 5-3); variations between specializations are roughly estimated from information about salaries.

derived from the marginal productivity theory of wages, whereby a profit-maximizing employer will not expand his workforce if an extra worker would add more to his costs than to his revenue. In a perfectly competitive labour market, thus, the wage is equal to productivity at the margin; hence the use of wages or earnings to measure productivity of benefit. However, the profit-maximizing calculus does not apply to all employers. The public sector, for instance, has quite different objectives, and some adjustment of public sector wages may be necessary for our purposes. And if, as is sometimes the case, labour markets are not perfectly competitive, the wage will be lower than marginal productivity even in the profit-maximizing sector.

Even if earnings broadly reflect productivity, not all of a differential in life-time earnings, between those who have been through a particular course and a control group who have not, is necessarily due to what has been learned on the course. In particular, social class, family background and academic potential or previous achievement may affect access to, performance in and the labour market consequences of education and training. This may not matter too much if social rates of return on courses with broadly comparable intakes are being compared but, otherwise, it may be important. For instance, comparisons between rates of return on academic schooling and those on vocational schooling are unfair if the control groups used do not reflect the differing backgrounds of the students at the two types of school. And rates of return on education need to be adjusted for this factor in comparisons with rates of return on non-educational investments.

There are also important indirect effects that are not captured by this measure and that have to be taken into account. On completion of their courses, graduates may be placed in jobs that were held by others up to that point or may fill vacancies that would have been filled by others in the absence of the training programme (the displacement effect). In the extreme case in which a trained worker merely bumps a less trained worker out of a job, taking over but not increasing the lifetime earnings stream associated with that job, the net social benefit from the training is zero. However, there may also be a replacement effect if the slot in the labour market vacated by the worker who joins the training programme and subsequently moves into a higher occupational category is filled by another worker who would otherwise have remained unemployed. This should be counted as an extra benefit. So too should the demonstration effect, whereby the skills acquired by trainees are later diffused to others who have not undergone the training; social effects, such as reductions in fertility levels; and dynamic effects, such as the opening up of employment opportunities for complementary workers who would otherwise be unemployed, the attraction of foreign investors and technology and the reduction in inflationary pressures.

All this means that planners of vocational education and training who follow this alternative approach have to use their informed judgement in deciding in which direction and roughly by how much their estimates of social rates of return on the programmes under review need to be modified. They have to get out of their offices and develop a "feel" for the relevant training programmes and labour markets by keeping in touch with educators, trainers, employers, employees, trainees, jobseekers and observers. They also have to become knowledgable about trends in technology and international product markets which will affect the future structure of the economy. And, in contrast to most manpower forecasting which aims at a one-off report, this has to be a continuous process; indicators have to be constantly updated as new information becomes available about rates of return and expected structural change. Clark (1986:138) calls it "an evolving procedure whereby appropriate and timely advice is constantly being fed into decision-making about education and training. The advice will change as new information becomes available, economic conditions change, or objectives are 'modified'".

A final advantage of this approach is that non-economic factors (not captured by rates of return) can easily be brought into the analysis. For instance, a government might decide that, in spite of a low current and prospective rate of return on training of architects, it wanted to build up a School of Islamic Architecture. The planners' responsibility in this case would be to point to the need to do something about the low private rate of return, for instance by commissioning the services of such architects, in order to attract good students who might otherwise choose other courses. In general, also, the approach draws attention to the cost, in terms of the higher rate of return forgone on other courses, of deciding to expand a programme purely on political grounds.

3. Summary of the role of the planner and of information needs

The idea of the planner as setter of precise targets was, in most countries, always something of a delusion; such targets, mercifully in view of their tenuous basis, have had very little influence on events. The role of the planner in the alternative approach outlined in this paper is more realistic – a collector and provider of information, a facilitator, an identifier of problems, an appraiser, an evaluator, and a nudger of institutions with long lead times in desirable directions.

Good information is, as always, the prerequisite of good planning. One reason for abandoning the old approach is that it has pretensions beyond the quality of its information base. The new approach is less pretentious, but its demands for high-quality data are alarming. In this final section an attempt will be made to identify the minimum set of information that is needed for this approach consistent with the capacity for regular data collection of government statistics departments.

Table 4.9 summarizes the methods of analysis and data needs and sources associated with each of the planning tasks.

An important function of planners of vocational education and training, already emphasized, is to disseminate information to people making decisions about occupations, courses and qualifications. Essentially (although they are unlikely to be aware of this terminology) they need to know which courses will give them the highest private rate of return. This defines the kind of information that needs to be collected and disseminated, information on fees and other private costs, earnings, degree of difficulty in obtaining jobs, and the expected implications of structural change for rates of return. This is the same kind of information that is needed for other purposes, but, for this purpose, it is important that it should be collected and published regularly.

The identification of problems and analysis of their causes, though based largely on informal talks with employers and other informants, will also be within a cost/outcome framework. Many of the indicators that are useful for this purpose will be routinely available from the publications or records of government departments — the civil service establishments section, the ministries of labour and education, the immigration department, the bureau of statistics, etc. Salary and other surveys carried out by consultancy firms may also be a useful source of information.

As for appraisal, monitoring and evaluation, in the case of short courses, it will be recalled, the hope is that the involvement of local employers in the management, design and finance of decentralized training institutions would help make them more flexible and responsive to the changing situation in local labour markets. Beyond this, appraisal of new projects and occasional monitoring and evaluation of existing ones through cost/outcome analysis would require information on costs, skill levels before and after courses, and labour market outcomes. This should be the kind of information that can be routinely collected by the training institutions themselves. However, procedures would have to be established and instruments designed (for instance, the reorganization of data on expenditure into a form that allows analysis of economic costs skill tests at the beginning and end of each course, questionnaires and procedures for regular tracing of graduates). Members of staff of the institutions would have to be trained

Table 4.9. Planning for vocational education and training: Methods, data needs and sources

	Methods of analysis	Data needs	Data sources
Collection and dissemination of information	Implicit private rate of return	Private costs. Earnings by occupation and qualification. Unemployment. Implications of structural change	Education/training institutions. Employers, workers, jobseekers, employment exchanges. Tracer studies
Identification of problems	Implicit cost/outcome	Information about problems affecting either cost or outcome. Labour market indicators	Informal talks with employers, trade unionists, researchers, educators, etc. Baseline studies. Government departments, consultancy firms
Analysis of causes	Cost/outcome	Information about problems affecting either cost or outcome, and opinions about their causes. Labour market indicators	Informal talks with employers, trade unionists, researchers, educators, etc. Baseline studies. Government departments, consultancy firms
Appraisal, monitoring and evaluation	Short courses: current rate of return	Estimated (for appraisal) or actual (for M & E) current and capital costs and skill and development outcomes	Education/training institutions. Workplaces and jobseekers
	Long courses: current rate of return and analysis of structural change	As above plus estimates of impact of structural change on rates of return	Education/training institutions. Workplace and jobseekers, tracer studies. Surveys of employment of graduates in this and a more advanced economy

in the collection of information for monitoring. Analysis of the information could be done centrally and the results returned to the institutions for comment and action.

For programmes with long lead times, the ideal approach, described above, involves tracer studies, of graduates from the programme in question and of control groups and analysis of the costs of the courses. As with the short courses, regular collection of basic data of this kind could be devolved to the training institutions themselves, with technical assistance and training from the planning agency. However, from time to time it may be useful for benchmark purposes to have a full-scale, centrally organized tracer study, along the lines of that of 1983 Malaysian graduates discussed above (Mehmet and Yip, 1986). Alongside this, the suggestion was of a survey of the employment of graduates of these and comparable courses in all sectors of the economy (with such subsectoral desegregation as might be required), and the collection of similar data from at least one other economy at a more advanced level of development. The purpose of these surveys would be more limited, with questions confined to details of qualifications, field of study, academic institution, and economic branch.[15]

[15] Estimating the impact of structural change on rates of return (for which these surveys are needed) will be most important in the case of appraisal of options for new long courses. For monitoring and evaluation, methods can be closer to those used for short courses, but the implications of future structural change will need to be taken into account in decisions about the redesign, continuation, expansion or replication of projects so evaluated.

This is a heavy programme of data collection, and it may be worth searching for short cuts that would ease the burden on training institutions, respondents and government statistics departments. One possibility would be to combine the purposes of the tracer studies and the survey of employment of graduates into a single survey administered to graduates in their workplaces or, in the case of unemployed jobseekers, through employment agencies, friends, etc., at intervals of a year or two. The streamlined version of the Malaysian Tracer Study Questionnaire (Appendix B) could be taken as a model, although most of the questions would only need to be asked and answered on the first occasion; on subsequent occasions updating alone would be required. A large sample and high response rate would be needed, for the reasons discussed above, but comfort can be derived from the fact that the survey would be confined to graduates of long courses.

To summarize, in the case of short courses, the emphasis would be on setting up structures and processes which ensured relevance and efficiency, putting training institutions virtually on automatic pilot. Such monitoring as might be required could largely be devolved to the institutions themselves. In the case of long courses, the statistical task might be described as the collection of data of high quality about a small part of the training system and labour market, in contrast to the manpower forecasters' practice of relying on data of poor quality about the whole of the labour market and as much of the training system as they could find. Undoubtedly, particularly in the early stages of the new approach, planners of vocational education and training would have to settle for using information that was less than perfect. But by asking the right questions they would at least be nudging collectors of information in the right direction.

The minimalist approach developed in this paper turns out to have something in common with the approach of those (e.g. Dougherty, 1986) who would like training systems to become largely self-regulating, with decisions about content and quantity in the hands of employers, and planners playing only a facilitating role. However, whatever the progress towards this goal (and it is likely to be slower than some of its advocates hope) the need to look forward to future directions for some types of vocational education and training will remain. A planning approach combining current rate of return analysis and analysis of expected structural change in the economy has been proposed for this purpose. Although the premise of the paper was the need to economize on scarce planning resources, minimalism will not necessarily mean less planning. What it will mean, as this paper has tried to show, is planning that is more interesting and, above all, more useful.

References

Ahamad, B. and M. Blaug. 1973. *The practice of manpower forecasting: A collection of case studies* (Amsterdam, Elsevier).

Amjad, R. 1985. *ARTEP's experience in short and medium term employment planning*, mimeo (New Delhi, ARTEP).

—. 1987. *Human resource planning: The Asian experience* (New Delhi, ILO/ARTEP).

Arcelo, A. A. and B. C. Sanyal. 1987. *Employment and career opportunities after graduation: The Philippine experience* (Manila, International Institute for Educational Planning/ Fund for Assistance to Private Education).

Bennell, P. 1980. *Engineering labour markets in Kenya* (Ph.D. thesis, University of Sussex).

Blaug, M. 1967. "Approaches to educational planning" in *Economic Journal*, June.

—. 1970. *An introduction to the economics of education* (London, Allen Lane, The Penguin Press).

—. 1981. *A UNIDO strategy for the training of industrial manpower in the third world*, mimeo (Vienna, UNIDO).

Clark, D. H. 1986. "Manpower planning – its contribution to vocational training planning" in *Indonesian Manpower Management Information System*.

Cohen, S.I. 1986. "Labour analysis and manpower planning: Examples from comprehensive technical cooperation programmes on human resources" in *Indonesian Manpower Management Information System*.

Crouch, L., M. Hopkins and S. Moreland, 1985. *MACBETH: A model for forecasting population, education, manpower, employment, underemployment and unemployment*, mimeo (Geneva).

Dougherty, C. 1983. "Manpower development from three points of view: Country, technical assistance agency, and lending agency" in Psacharopoulos et al.

—. 1986. "Technological change and manpower development planning" in *Indonesian Manpower Management Information System*.

—. 1990. *Education and skill development: Planning issues*, Asian Development Bank/World Bank Seminar on Vocational and Technical Education and Training (Manila) January.

Godfrey, M. 1987. *Planning for education, training and employment*. Summary Report, UNDP/ILO Project INS/84/006 (Jakarta).

Government of Israel, Central Bureau of Statistics. 1988. *Survey of graduates of universities and post-secondary education 1984*, Special Series No. 820 (Jerusalem).

Hollister, R. 1967. *Technical evaluation of the first stage of the Mediterranean regional project* (Paris, OECD).

Hunting, G., M. Zymelman and M. Godfrey. 1986. *Evaluating vocational training programmes: A practical guide* (Washington, DC, World Bank).

Indonesian Manpower Management Information System. 1986. *Report on the seminar: New orientations of manpower planning and analysis and their relevance to Indonesia*, ILO/UNDP Project INS/85/034 (Jakarta).

ILO/APSDEP. 1988. *Training of technicians for the mechatronics age* (Islamabad, APSDEP).

Jolly, R. and C. Colclough. 1972. "African manpower plans: An evaluation" in *International Labour Review*, 106:2-3, August-September.

Leibenstein, H. 1957. *Economic backwardness and economic growth* (New York, John Wiley and Sons).

Malaysian Industrial Development Authority in collaboration with UNIDO. 1985. *Medium and long term industrial master plan: Malaysia*, Vol. 111, Part 5, Manpower and Training, August (Kuala Lumpur).

Mehmet, O. and Yip Yat Hoong. 1986. *Human capital formation in Malaysian universities: A socio-economic profile of the 1983 graduates*, Occasional Papers and Reports, No. 2 (Kuala Lumpur, University of Malaya, Institute of Advanced Studies).

Psacharopoulos, G. et al. 1983. *Manpower issues in educational investment, a consideration of planning processes and techniques* (Washington, DC, World Bank).

Psacharopoulos, G. and M. Woodhall. 1985. *Education for development: Analysis of investment choices* (New York, Oxford University Press).

Sanyal, B.C., L. Yaici, and I. Mallasi. 1987. *From college to work: The case of the Sudan* (Paris, International Institute for Educational Planning).

Statistics Canada. 1989. *Follow-up of 1982 graduates: Survey methodology report and user's guide* (Ottawa).

World Bank. *Vocational education and training in developing countries: Policies for flexibility, efficiency and quality* (Washington, DC, forthcoming).

Zymelman, M. 1984. *Occupational structures of industries* (Washington, DC, World Bank).

Appendix A
Some recent tracer studies

The most ambitious of recent tracer studies is the 1987 survey of the labour market experience of 1982 graduates from Canadian universities, community colleges and trade/vocational programmes (Statistics Canada, 1989). This was a follow-up to a survey of the same cohort of graduates in 1984 and to a 1978 survey of 1976 graduates. Data were collected by telephone interview from a sample of almost 36,000 graduates; an overall response rate of 89 per cent was achieved. Nine major field of study strata were used for university programmes, nine for career/technical programmes and ten for trade/vocational programmes. The questionnaire contained a total of 113 questions, covering details of occupations, related work experience, educational requirements for jobs, job satisfaction, remuneration, job search activities, education, training, relationship between education and work and other demographic and social issues, but no respondent had to answer all questions. The questions most relevant to our purpose concern qualifications (What types of degrees, diplomas or certificates have you obtained?), field of study, family background (What is the highest level of education completed by your father and by your mother or guardian?), and remuneration (if you were to work at your job for the 12 months of 1987, approximately what would be your gross earnings?).

Much more modest in scale and purpose was a survey of final year secondary school and higher education students, university graduates and employers, carried out in the Sudan in the early 1980s (Sanyal et al., 1987). The sample of graduates covered by the survey was only 500, mostly from the classes of 1967-74, and the response rate was only 69 per cent. The questionnaire contained 36 questions, covering personal characteristics, educational history (including attitudes, motives and awards), field of study (twelve broad categories), match between higher education and job, job search, opinions about suitable arrangements to make higher education more responsive to the world of work, motives for migration, opinions about suitable arrangements for graduate placement and about incentives and disincentives to work in rural areas, and job satisfaction. There were no questions about remuneration

In the 1981 survey of 1979-1981 graduates in the Philippines (Arcelo and Sanyal, 1987) the sample was larger, at 2,598, but the response rate, at 49 per cent, was even lower. The questionnaire contained 49 questions, covering personal characteristics, family background (including parents' occupation, industry and income as well as education), details of education and training (including reasons for choice of course and assessment of performance and quality), employment (by type of firm,

Table A.1. Field of study strata and specific degrees used in Malaysian tracer study

(a) *Arts, Humanities and Social Sciences*
Arts
Arts (Honours)
Arts with Education
Islamic Studies
Islamic Studies (Honours)
Social Science
Social Science (Honours)
Education (Agricultural Science) (Honours)
Education (Home Technology) (Honours)
Education (Physical Education) (Honours)

(b) *General Science*
Science with Education
Science with Education (Honours)
Science
Science (Honours)
Applied Science (Honours)
Science (Human Development) (Honours)

(c) *Economics and Business Administration*
Business Administration
Business Administration (Honours)
Economics
Accounting (Honours)
Science (Resource Economics) (Honours)

(d) *Law*
L.L.B. (Honours)

(e) *Health Science*
M.B.B.S.
Pharmacy (Honours)
Dental Surgery
Veterinary Medicine

(f) *Agricultural Sciences*
Agricultural Science (Honours)
Food Science and Technology (Honours)
Science (Fishery) (Honours)
Science (Agri-business) (Honours)
Science (Forestry) (Honours)

(g) *Architecture, Surveying, Urban and Regional Planning*
Surveying
Surveying (Honours)
Architecture (Honours)
Surveying (Property Management) (Honours)
Urban and Regional Planning
Urban and Regional Planning (Honours)
Science (Housing, Building and Planning) (Honours)
Science (Environment) (Honours)

(h) *Engineering*
Engineering (Agriculture)
Engineering (Civil)
Engineering (Civil) (Honours)
Engineering (Petroleum) (Honours)
Engineering (Electrical) (Honours)
Engineering (Mechanical) (Honours)
Engineering (Chemical) (Honours)

Source: Mehmet and Yip (1986: Table 3-5).

occupation, industry, average monthly salary before tax deduction, and regular work-ing hours per week, excluding overtime), other sources and size of income, previous work experience, job search, field of specialization (24 categories – see Table 4.1 above) and relevance to current job, and job satisfaction.

The final survey to be summarized here, carried out in Malaysia in August-September 1984, aimed for a sample of 2,278 (half the graduating cohort of 1983) and achieved a response rate of 89 per cent. The questionnaire contained 34 questions, covering personal characteristics (including ethnic origin), educational background (distinguishing 37 fields of study, and within many of them distinguishing honours from other degrees – see Table A1), family characteristics (including parents' educa-tion, ownership of assets, employment, occupation, income and family income from all sources), cost of university education and method of finance, and details of current labour force status (including, if employed, occupation, type of firm, starting and pre-sent pre-tax monthly salary including bonuses, tips and allowances).

Appendix B
A streamlined version of the Malaysian tracer study questionnaire

To be filled by enumerator:

Date of survey _____

University _____

Name of enumerator _____

University code _____

To be filled by overchecker:

Name _____

Data _____

Questionnaire no. _____

I. Personal and family characteristics of the graduate

1. Full name of graduate _____

2. Degree received _____ Pass/honours _____
   Class _____
   Faculty _____

3. Main subject of specialization _____

4. Postal address _____
   _____
   _____ tel. _____ ext. _____

5. Age on 1st February 1983 _____ (to nearest year)

6. Sex
   Male _____ 1   Female _____ 2

7. Ethnic origin
   Malay __1   Indian __ 3   Iban __ 5   Other E. Malaysian __ 7
   Chinese __ 2   Ceylonese __ 4   Kadazan __ 6   Others __ 8

8. Give the highest educational attainment of your parents (or guardians):

	Father	*Mother*	*Guardian*
Holds university degree	01	01	01
Some university education	02	02	02
Completed non-university tertiary level (e.g. technical school)	03	03	03
Some non-university tertiary level	04	04	04
Completed secondary school (Form V)	05	05	05
Some secondary school	06	06	06
Completed primary school (Std 6)	07	07	07
Some primary school	08	08	08
Village religious school	09	09	09
No formal schooling	10	10	10

II. Financing your education

9. How many years of study did it take you to get your Bachelor degree?
Three __ 1   Five __ 3   Seven __ 5
Four __ 2   Six __ 4   More than seven __ 6

10. Give the breakdown of the **average annual cost** of your university education, including amounts paid out of scholarships (if you were receiving one). Compute your **average cost** over the entire period of university education.

Average annual cost (to the nearest $100)

i.	Tuition	$ _____
ii.	Books, supplies and equipment	$ _____
iii.	Food and clothing	$ _____
iv.	Residence or rented accommodation	$ _____
v.	Transportation to university	$ _____
vi.	Others (please specify) _____	$ _____
	TOTAL	$ _____

11. How was your university education financed?

By whom or how? Source	Annual amount or	% age of average annual costs
i. Parents/guardian	$ _____	$ _____
ii. Scholarship/bursary/grant:		
(a) Government (Federal/State)	$ _____	$ _____
or (b) Statutory body	$ _____	$ _____
or (c) Private firm	$ _____	$ _____
or (d) Others (specify) _____	$ _____	$ _____
iii. Borrowings:		
(a) Relatives and friends	$ _____	$ _____
(b) Student loan funds	$ _____	$ _____
(c) Government/statutory body	$ _____	$ _____
(d) Others (specify)	$ _____	$ _____
iv. Own savings	$ _____	$ _____
v. Others (specify) _____	$ _____	$ _____
TOTAL	$ _____	$ _____

12. If you were awarded a scholarship/bursary/grant:
i. Were you bonded by it?   Yes _____ No _____
ii. State the number of years of bond _____
iii. What was the amount of penalty to discharge it? $ _____

III. Current labour force status of graduates

13. Are you working now?
Working full time _____ 1
Working part time _____ 2
Not working _____ 3 (go to question 20)

14. How soon after completing your requirements for graduation did you start working?
Immediately _____ 1
Within 2 months _____ 2
Within 2-6 months _____ 3

15. What is your exact job title or occupation? _____

16. Is this your first, second or third job?
    First __1   Third __3
    Second __2   Fourth __4

17. What is your employment status?
    Employee of government __1   Employee of private firm __3
    Employee of statutory body __2   Self-employed __4
    Employer __5

18. Name and address of employer:
    _____
    _____
    _____

19. What was your starting salary in your first job after graduation (including all tips, allowances, etc.) **before tax**?
    $_____ (per month)

20. What is your **present** monthly salary?
    $_____ (per month)

Note: The following questions are applicable only if you are currently unemployed:

21. If you are now unemployed, are you actively looking for a job
    (e.g. applying for vacancies)?
    Yes __1   No __2

22. If No, give the reasons:
    Housewife/mother __1   Further studies __2
    Other (explain) _____

Source: Adapted from Mehmet and Yip (1986: Appendix A).

5

The role of manpower planning in Africa in current widespread crisis conditions

Eleazar C. Iwuji*

1. Introduction

Manpower planning has been adopted by most African countries since the early 1960s. It was particularly the case when many African countries became politically independent and wanted to prepare their nationals for posts in the public service held until then by foreigners, but found themselves faced with many problems such as an inadequate stock of human resources. The need to "Africanize" as rapidly as possible necessitated the "stocktaking" of skilled personnel by occupation and nationality to determine the existing gaps. With the introduction of long-term development plans (for most of the countries, their first) there was a subsequent need to determine the likely degree of localization. And with localization, there was the wish of most States to build or expand universities, for which quantitative guidelines were required. At the same time, the educational planners were under considerable pressure to expand educational opportunities to their own nationals and provide the skills required for implementing the development programmes. In some cases, pressure was extended by bilateral agencies and international organizations seeking knowledge of the current manpower situation and likely future demand for the purpose of development assistance in the fields of education, training and fellowships.

Manpower planning offered a measure for localization, a method of educational planning, and a means of quantifying or justifying technical training to produce skills for an expanding modern sector.

2. Manpower planning: The African experience

Manpower planning is conceived as a mechanism for matching skill requirements (labour demand) to development plan targets. The objectives of manpower planning can be said to be twofold.[1] The first is to assess the needs for skilled human resources of the economy within a certain period in order to determine to what

* International Labour Office.

[1] Amjad (ed.), 1989.

extent the production of skills will satisfy the anticipated demand and suggest poss-ible measures for reducing the supply/demand imbalances. The second objective is to provide an analytical framework which in human resources planning will serve as a guideline for educational planning and investment allocation to education, training and manpower development.

The actual task of achieving these objectives, manpower planning practice in Africa, faced serious difficulties from the start. The basic data on population, labour force, participation rates, employment output from educational and training institu-tions, gross domestic product, productivity, etc., were largely absent. There was a shortage of funds, staff and facilities for conducting even simple establishment enquiries. Under such circumstances comprehensive manpower planning was not feasible. Manpower planning exercises were confined to such attempts as: collection of available information on the existing stock and likely supply of manpower and rough estimate of likely future demands. Detailed projections of manpower needs over a long period could not be attempted.

The JASPA 1983/84 country studies covering sub-Saharan Africa throw considerable light into the way in which manpower planning has been attempted, the preoccupation with manpower forecasting and the weaknesses of the conven-tional approaches adopted. More importantly they raise the question of whether the approaches have guided decision-makers in resource allocation for skill develop-ment programmes.

Manpower planning has traditionally dealt with the identification of skill requirements, and the identification of skills still seems to be the main function of manpower planning in Africa. The assumption was that there was little flexibility, therefore the right number of say, engineers or technicians, university graduates or secondary school-leavers had to be educated to achieve production targets or expand economic growth.[2] These forecasts were concerned about avoiding shortages and in Africa they were closely associated with localization programmes. Manpower requirements and their translation into specific educational training requirements became particularly attractive to newly independent African countries.

Method of manpower forecasting

There is no single method of forecasting manpower requirements. The stan-dard methodology most commonly used is based on the manpower requirements approach which links requirements with anticipated levels of output for each indus-try sector or the whole economy.

The earliest attempts (and in fact for Nigeria following the Ashby Report in Nigeria)[3] were based on simple "rules of thumb". The assumption was that high-level manpower should grow twice as fast as the target rate of economic growth and that intermediate manpower should grow three times as fast. These rules were not based on evidence or analysis but on conjecture. But as real doubts began to arise when

[2] Psacharopoulos and Woodham, 1985.
[3] Ashby, 1960.

forecasts proved to be inaccurate and unreliable as a basis for the planning of education and training programmes, countries turned to other techniques, namely:

- employers' estimates of future manpower requirements;
- international comparisons;
- rate of return analysis;
- manpower population ratios; and
- extrapolation of fixed input-output ratios.

While it is not intended here to go into the details of each of these manpower forecasting techniques and the controversies associated with each (which are
too well known and documented to be repeated) it must be stated that each has its
distinct concepts, areas of application, merits and demerits and different data
requirements. They nearly all attempt to project present employment according to
the behaviour of the various parameters which influence future levels and patterns of
employment. The projections are intended to provide guidelines for policy in terms
of new job places required or skilled manpower needed over plan periods.[4] What is
perhaps of primary interest here is the fact that because of unreliability and unsuit-
ability and the inability of manpower forecasting to change with changing development priorities, there have been increasing doubts about the validity of the techniques for forecasting overall manpower requirements.

It must, however, be admitted that this has hardly reduced the appeal and
popularity of the manpower requirements approach with many policymakers and
planners in Africa.

3. Changes in development strategies

In the past two decades (1970s-80s) conventional manpower planning has,
however, been overtaken by dramatic changes in development strategies. The rapid
expansion in education had not been matched by the optimistic targets set in the
1960s and early 1970s for economic growth and employment. Traditional economic
strategy had concentrated on economic growth (i.e. rapid gains in overall and per
capita GNP growth) and the expectation was that the benefits of such growth would
"trickle down" to the mass of the population. Experience, however, showed that this
was not the case, for in many countries not only did the poor remain poor but high
growth rates were often accompanied by increased inequality. The 1970s experienced
widespread dislocations. The changing oil prices, boom and bust in commodity
prices, and overburdening of debt affected most countries in the world. The sub-
Saharan and African region's ability to adjust to these new economic realities was
greatly weakened by its extraordinarily limited policy analytic and management
capacity. It became clear that development strategy should not just be preoccupied
with the growth of aggregate output but with a more equal distribution of income and
alleviation of poverty. The rapid decline in infant mortality, the subsequent increase

[4] Richter, 1989.

in school-age population and labour force together with strong social demand for education and wage employment highlighted the broader labour market issues. The concern of planners thus shifted to the question of how to avoid surpluses and how to reduce unemployment. Emphasis was increasingly placed on employment-oriented development rather than growth-oriented strategies and by mid-1970s on reducing inequality through employment-creation and through the provision of "basic needs". Development plans thus stressed the need to reduce poverty and achieve a more even distribution of incomes, as well as increasing the supply of high-level manpower to implement major development programmes in key sectors.

There was also the change in the attitudes towards the planning of education. As many educationists seriously questioned the idea of education being for the purpose of improving economic efficiency, the view that education has many non-vocational benefits was increasingly shared by policymakers. This viewpoint, together with the growing school-age population and "social demand" for education following the general perception that schooling was an avenue to better paid jobs, put enormous pressure on planners to rapidly expand enrolments.

In the 1980s, the combined external shocks of higher interest rates, increased oil prices, worldwide recession, declining terms of trade and a serious debt-burden, forced many developing countries to adopt IMF/World Bank-inspired structural adjustment programmes. These developments called for changes towards export-oriented manufacturing industries, reduction in public expenditure, maintenance of competitive wage rates, measures to attract foreign investment and adoption of new technologies.

The shift in development policy had enormous implications for manpower planning and training policies and should have been accompanied with similar shifts in manpower policy. Instead too many manpower planning units have continued their traditional task of adopting the manpower requirement approach for making forecasts of skill requirements which have become outmoded if not irrelevant in the light of rapid changes in the labour market and development strategies, both for medium- and long-term planning.

The National Manpower Decree 1991[5] recently promulgated in Nigeria is very illustrative of the situation. The National Manpower Board when first established in Nigeria in mid-1960 was given the overall responsibility for employment and manpower. The Board was reconstituted by Decree No. 18 of 30th May 1991 but is still charged with the same principal function that it had performed since its inception namely, "to determine and advise the Government on the nation's manpower needs in all occupations".[6] Thus, the only new thing about the Decree, as a recent report on Nigeria rightly observed:

> is that the Decree now gives the Board an autonomous status as a Parastatal, and the needed flexibility, and hopefully a greater claim to resources to facilitate execution of its functions.

---

[5] *Federal Republic of Nigeria Official Gazette*, 1991.
[6] Ukwu et al., 1991.

On the dogged adherence of the Government (as in most governments in Africa) to manpower requirement approach, the report concludes:

> The activities of the National Manpower Board have in the past concentrated on manpower planning in the classical sense. Neither, the Manpower Secretariat nor the Federal Ministry of Employment had done any serious employment planning.[7]

4. The impact of conventional manpower planning on policy

The efficacy of manpower planning may be judged by how much its approaches have guided decision-makers in resource allocation for skill development programmes and its impact on policies in general. Judged on the basis of the above, the impact of manpower planning on policy formulation in Africa can for a number of reasons be said to be minimal.

In many African countries a communication gulf seems to exist between manpower planners and decision-makers which suggests that either the use of manpower planning is not fully understood or that decision-makers, do not see manpower planning as a useful instrument for planning purposes. Both arguments can be justified. In the former case, it is known that civil servants do not seem well informed about the activities of manpower planning either in its conventional role of forecasting manpower requirements or in its expanded role of developing human resources. In the latter case, there are also many instances in educational planning where manpower considerations were neglected either on the grounds of social reasons (e.g. the introduction of universal primary education programmes) or political (e.g. the establishment of a second university, and, in the Nigerian case, state universities in addition to federal universities). It must also be admitted that policy in the human resources field is influenced by many other factors apart from those that a manpower planner might recommend. Furthermore, in a highly politicized system the probability of the manpower planner being overruled is very high indeed.

The influence of manpower planners seems also to have been greatly minimized by the lack of confidence on the part of senior government officials. This lack of confidence can be attributed to the lack of understanding of planning techniques, past inaccuracies and the excessively quantitative approach to educational planning. Thus although many educational planners have claimed the need for advice from manpower planners on specific requirements in various disciplines, in reality, they have been known to be very sceptical about the methodology used for forecasting. Perhaps much more serious is the lack of dialogue between manpower and educational planners, but such dialogue is an essential stage in any planning process. Similarly, the fact that manpower planners are rarely in a position to dictate to the Ministry of Education and the universities (nor should they) has not helped matters or enhanced their influence. Finally, there is the all-important question of what the

[7] ibid., p. 31.

main objectives of manpower planning should be and for what purposes. Inadequate attention had been given to this question and, as a result, many of the countries did not have a clearly thought-out manpower policy; manpower planning functions and programmes had not been linked to national development objectives, nor integrated into the mainstream of national planning. Rather the manpower section of a national plan often seemed to have been added as an annex.

Concern with manpower forecasting may have been justified in the 1960s when, as has been noted, localization was the dominant policy issue among newly independent countries but localization was essentially the once-for-all replacement of expatriates. By the 1970s, a high level of localization had been achieved, if not in certain skill areas, then overall and had ceased to be a major issue for most African countries with a growing school population, an increase in the social demand for education and an expanding labour force and shifts in priority on development issues. The changed situations in the 1970s and 1980s have thus reduced the relevance of the manpower requirement approach as an important tool for planning purposes. If manpower planning is to be an instrument of planning it must adapt its functions and responsibilities as the concerns of policymakers change.

5. The case of manpower analysis

The realization that manpower planning is not simply a matter of matching supply to demand balances, or taking decisions on how much to invest in education, but the outcome of a much more complex exercise (involving a number of factors which defy simplistic manpower forecasting) has led to the recognition of the need for an alternative framework and the orientation towards manpower analysis.

While conventional manpower planning is concerned primarily with preparing quantitative projections, and is one step in the formulation of the overall development plan, manpower analysis emphasizes manpower planning as a continuous process and requires regular feedback, updating, continuous analysis, and monitoring rather than preparation of occasional quantitative projections.[8] It concentrates on the understanding of labour market and of processes which essentially determine the manner in which demand signals are finally communicated and the supply response to them. The emphasis is thus on regular analysis of data so as to reveal trends in manpower utilization and the relationships between education and employment.

The subject of manpower analysis is thus the wide variety of factors that influence labour market transactions and manpower allocation practices, both in formal and in informal labour markets. It is by such analysis that the employment process can be identified and monitored and its dynamics and transactions understood. In other words, the analysis of current and past patterns of manpower utilization is likely to provide more information on the operation of the labour market than simple projections of past manpower trends.

The effectiveness of manpower planning and labour market analysis very much depends on a sound information base. Similarly, the formulation of employ-

---

[8] See Psacharopoulos and Woodham, op. cit.; Richer, op. cit.

ment and manpower planning and the translation of the same into the generation of employment very much depend on the establishment of labour market information systems to support the activities of decision-makers and planners. In other words, the availability of a reliable, comprehensive and up-to-date LMI system, to analyse and assess the changing employment situation and employment and manpower needs, is a necessary condition for successful employment and manpower planning and implementation.

Labour market information (LMI) in sub-Saharan Africa

Although African countries have been very concerned about unemployment, there was until fairly recently an apparent lack of understanding among policy-makers and planners of the usefulness of labour market information for a variety of decision-making purposes, such as determining manpower training needs, identifying the availability of labour, ascertaining prevailing wage rates and exploring potential markets, etc.

Now there is, however, an increasing recognition among the countries of the need for comprehensive labour market information covering all sectors, occupational groups and geographical areas of the country as a purposeful tool for decision-making and programme planning in all matters relating to manpower and employment policy.

Even so, the establishment of a comprehensive LMI system has not made much progress in most of the countries. Reference to the status of LMI in a few countries in Africa may provide more information. A recent multi-sectoral needs assessment team mission to Nigeria (July 1991) observed as follows:

> The activities of the National Manpower Board have in the past concentrated on manpower planning in the classical sense. Neither the Manpower Secretariat nor the Federal Ministry of Employment had done any serious employment planning.[9]

The situation in a number of other countries is similar or even worse. In Sierra Leone the institutional arrangement for monitoring the employment situation and advising on appropriate employment and manpower development policy does not exist in any of the line ministries nor are any of the ministries in a position to provide reliable, comprehensive and up-to-date information and data on the labour market situation and employment.[10] In Uganda, LMI is among the least articulated subjects in both development planning and approaches to employment issues.[11] In Ethiopia, though a lot of labour market data exist, they are scattered and unorganized. They are limited both in scope and coverage since they were designed to accomplish a particular purpose. "Therefore, it is hard to say that LMI collected so far is comprehensive and complete or particularly useful".[12] Zimbabwe

[9] Ukwu et al., op. cit.
[10] ILO/JASPA, 1990.
[11] ILO/JASPA, 1989.
[12] Badada, 1986.

has since 1980 attempted to collect a better quality of LMI related to the immediate and medium-term policy needs of her human resource development programme but there are still serious lacunas in the collection of data.[13] Zambia has been described as one of the few African countries which has a well organized and fairly developed statistical system possessing more LMI than many African countries;[14] but a lot of the LMI collected is scattered and not well coordinated. The United Republic of Tanzania is in several respects far behind some of its neighbouring countries such as Kenya, Zambia and Zimbabwe as far as establishing a comprehensive and reliable LMI system goes, but not completely oblivious of the need for evolving a LMI programme.[15]

Probably no country in sub-Saharan Africa has yet achieved a comprehensive, updated and reliable LMI system. Similarly, despite the awareness among employers' and workers' organizations of the need for LMI, particularly on such subjects as wages, prices, conditions of work, training facilities and industrial relations, which they themselves need for bargaining, few of them have developed LMI programmes of their own. Employers' organizations appear, however, to be relatively more aware of the need for starting LMI work than workers' organizations; and in a few countries have or are in the process of setting up an economic research programme of their own for the benefit of their members.

While many of the countries can be said to be at different stages of developing LMI programmes, certain features or characteristics, particularly problems and constraints which limit the usefulness of LMI, appear fairly common among them.

These relate to the types of LMI collected, which suffer from serious gaps and inadequacies, and techniques used for analysis – the major pitfalls being in (a) data gathering, collection and collation, and (b) processing, analysis and dissemination of data.

There are also organizational constraints which are evidenced in:

A dearth of experts and trained staff: Arrangements and facilities for the systematic training of relevant staff in technical and organizational skills needed for LMI programmes are absent in most of the countries, often owing to a lack of financial resources. The allocation of resources for the development of LMI programmes has not in many countries been recognized as an item deserving special consideration in the budgetary allocation. In effect, the practice has been to leave it to the ministries' or agencies' discretion to decide what amount to devote to LMI activities. This invariably results in a serious shortage of expertise and trained staff required for the successful and effective operations of LMI programmes. Limited financial resources are also reflected in the inability to purchase modern processing equipments such as micro-computers and the necessary software, etc., in order to keep abreast with modern technology and new techniques.

Coordination of LMI: The coordination of the contributions from various sources towards a labour market information programme is a crucial function and

---

[13] Raftopoulos, 1986.
[14] Nigam, 1988a.
[15] Nigam, 1988b.

should be entrusted to a suitable national agency. The main tasks of such coordinating body or agency should be to rationalize the collection and compilation of information, undertake its analysis, and develop procedures for an integrated system of collection of data on LMI programmes. It should also monitor the progress of each stage of the national labour market and ensure dissemination of LMI. In many of the countries such machinery is either weak or does not exist.

The lack of an appropriate LMI system has thus contributed to the ineffectiveness and decline of manpower planning. The LMI systems have not provided the data in the form needed by planners to assess the key issues in the labour market. They have been mostly too fragile to support serious analytical policy-oriented studies.[16]

6. Implications of developments in macroeconomic policies for manpower planning in Africa: Structural adjustment programmes [17]

The adoption of structural adjustment programmes and the transition to a different type of economy presented most African countries with a new set of challenges with respect to manpower and employment issues. Among these are unemployment pressures on public sector employment, the need for direct employment creation, the impact of structural adjustment on labour markets, recession and slower growth, the assessment of skill needs, public sector manpower, etc. In the adverse state of prolonged economic contraction and uncertainty, employment and manpower planning has, at least in the short term, been thrown into confusion. In the process of change the hardest hit have been the poorest sections of the population. Many countries have had to reorient their development planning towards short-term priorities and targets at sectoral and subsectoral levels.

These factors, of which unemployment seems the most serious, have important implications for skill formation and the reorientation of existing education and training systems – all the more so, with the growing emphasis on the "demand" side of human resources planning, especially the problem of short-term employment creation, rapid urbanization, urban employment and the informal sector.[18] These developments call for effective programmes and policies on manpower and employment planning (human resources development). There is a need for an integrated approach towards manpower and employment planning in order to ensure efficiency in human resources allocation. The close links between human capital and economic development demand a broad-based and comprehensive approach. For the same reason, employment and manpower planning should be fully integrated into the overall development planning process. The essence of this approach is to ensure that while critical human resource requirements of the development plan are met in time, there should be no underutilization of this resource because such underutilization

---

[16] Nigam, ibid.

[17] This section relies heavily on ILO/JASPA: *Guidelines and methodological approaches to human resources planning in Africa* (Addis Ababa, 1989).

[18] ILO/JASPA, 1989.

would amount to economic loss and loss of human well-being. In this regard, labour market information is of crucial importance. Its ability to adopt to changes in demand and price changes can positively affect the whole economy in utilizing the opportunities which may open up as macroeconomic management and stabilization policies are improved.

In the short term, the manpower planner should examine policies related to self-employment, high concentrations of unemployment and poverty levels. National development plans usually show that both in the short and long term this is often not reflected in sectoral plans and projects. In the longer term macroeconomic policies to stimulate economic growth and employment creation should be assessed.

The manpower planner should not only examine the consequences of structural adjustment on human resources but also how human resources can assist structural adjustment. Even under structural adjustment careful employment and manpower analysis can assist in meeting the objectives of economic growth, structural transformation, employment promotion and optimal human resources development. Although it will be necessary to be conscious of the impact of structural adjustment on the labour market vis-à-vis falling real wages, reduction in labour standards and the increase in insecure and low wage jobs, since structural adjustment programmes are designed to stimulate economic development, increased labour mobility and changes in labour legislation should be encouraged. Manpower planners in assessing the impact of structural adjustment policies on employment should remember that while such policies will initially result in retrenchments in both the public and private sectors, successful implementation of such policies will eventually lead to employment creation.

Manpower requirements

A major concern of the manpower planner is the provision of skills to meet changes in the industrial sector (towards export-led industries) so that the process of structural adjustment is not hindered by shortages of skilled manpower. To avoid a situation where serious skill shortages pose a threat to domestic and foreign investment, manpower planners will have to anticipate rapidly changing skill requirements in key sectors of the economy, particularly the quality of the labour force, which to a great extent influence foreign investment. In view of the difficulty in anticipating the new patterns of demand for the suppliers and skilled manpower, this assessment work is better and more effectively done at the subsectoral level.

The likely possibility of skill mismatches because of the expected rapid changes in the industrial structure demands that the manpower planner should increasingly give more attention to employment information services (labour market information) and flexibility of training programmes in both the public and private sectors and the improvement of "in-plant" training.

Assessment of skill needs

The need for the provision of skills to meet shifts in the industrial sector, so that the process of structural change is not constrained by shortages of skilled manpower, is overwhelming. This for the manpower planner will entail determining the skilled manpower requirements in the different subsectors and at the different levels, and, in particular, the most critical skills needed and the most effective and expeditious ways and means of meeting these needs. Some countries have surpluses in educated manpower and apparently do not seem to suffer from skill shortage problems. Some, however, suffer from shortages of skilled manpower. Although a national assessment of manpower needs seems to have been preferred as a guide to the planning of the education and training sector, it has to be accepted that the methods of forecasting have not been sufficiently reliable to justify the cost of such an exercise. The unstable economic conditions in the past two decades have thrown development plans into such disarray that detailed manpower planning has also suffered.

Sectoral approach

The adoption of structural adjustment has provided a strong impetus for the orientation of manpower planning towards sectors. For the specific effects and implications of structural adjustment on employment and manpower planning to be properly observed and handled early enough to avoid undesirable developments, the sectoral approach to manpower planning should be adopted instead of concentrating exclusively on nationwide and macro-manpower planning. The sectoral approach should be encouraged particularly with respect to the different economic sectors and the public and private sectors.

Sectoral employment and manpower planning approaches are justified not only on the grounds of a lack of adequate nationwide data but also by the fact that the adverse effects of structural adjustment have reduced the traditional role of the public sector as a chief provider of jobs (particularly, for higher skill categories) in the majority of African countries. Sectoral employment and manpower planning also assist in exploring possibilities of redeploying manpower, especially in those public sector activities which have met with severe cuts in public expenditure. At the sectoral level data needs are simpler and the manpower planner should be able to identify key (as opposed to all) skill shortages and the resources for eliminating the shortages, identify training priorities, advise on the allocation of funds for training purposes, evaluate the efficiency of training establishments and consult employers. Attention should also be increasingly turned to the manpower requirements of the productive sectors of the economy, notably industry and agriculture, to exploit more fully their latent employment potential, as well as how to increase their employment potential compared to the past.

Public sector manpower

As already mentioned, recession and adjustment policies have had serious adverse effects for the public sector, which until fairly recently was more used to creating employment for high level manpower than shedding off labour and redeploying redundant manpower (as a result of cutbacks in public expenditure). No matter what methods are employed, e.g. early retirement or wage cuts, to reduce public sector expenditure, there will be a need to carefully monitor changes taking place in the structure and size of the civil service as well as the components of the wage bill to ensure that performance and efficiency do not suffer.

Similarly, in order to attract and retain the skills necessary for the public sector's role in supporting structural adjustments development, governments may have to reflect skill scarcity by, in effect, permitting an increase in real wages for the "hard-to-gct" skills, and to review recruitment policy.

Private sector

With the adoption of the structural adjustment programmes in many countries, the increasingly important objective for the manpower planner is to shift the concentration from the public sector, which in terms of employment has reached saturation point, to the needs of the private sector.

In this connection, it has been suggested[19] that the manpower planner considers measures to channel people into: (i) jobs where manpower is required and (ii) with appropriate industrial training schemes and also (iii) to improve performance of industrial manpower in filling skill shortages. The main issues to consider are the role of the employment services, recruitment policies and attempts to reverse any "brain drain". For training schemes, manpower planners should consider vocational guidance for high-level industrial manpower, especially selected strategic occupations, improved data on industrial occupations and improved selection processes (especially aptitude tests). On improving the performance of the industrial labour force, the measures should include rationalizing the organization of industrial firms (staffing patterns, shiftwork and ineffective time) and developing patterns of incentives.

7. Conclusion

The conventional manpower approach has been the goal of macroeconomic policy for many African countries and still retains its appeal and popularity among them despite its many drawbacks and the general disenchantment with its approach to educational planning.

The changed situations in the 1970s and 1980s, particularly the adoption of structural adjustment programmes are, however, reducing the relevance of the man-

---

[19] ILO/JASPA, 1989.

power requirements approach as an important tool for planning purposes and gradually leading to a new orientation and approach in the practice of manpower planning.

Manpower planning should be more meaningfully and usefully seen as an integrated approach to human resources development, highlighting the interrelationships between investment in education and skill development as well as the creation of gainful employment. It should also be seen as providing the analytical basis from which appropriate decisions on investment in education, training and human resources development can be made rather than as an exercise in projecting requirements of demand and supply and adjusting accordingly.

There is therefore the need for manpower planning to become an integral part of the overall development strategy and not an annex to it.

This emerging new awareness amounts to a convergence of the understanding of the function of market analysis and LMI that will eventually displace traditional manpower planning and hopefully enthrone employment and manpower planning.

Manpower analysis emphasizes manpower planning as a continuous process and requires regular feedback, updating, continuous analysis and monitoring rather than the preparation of occasional quantitative projections.

The effectiveness of manpower planning and labour market analysis depends on a sound information base and the understanding of how labour markets function. This requires the establishment of reliable, comprehensive and up-to-date LMI systems as a necessary condition in order to support the activities of decision-makers and planners.

Existing sources of LMI sources in African countries are far from satisfactory. They suffer from serious gaps and inadequacies. Investments of public resources to overcome these will be socially justifiable.

There is need to significantly strengthen the institutional machinery engaged in employment and manpower planning. This should include the enhancement of the technical capability of personnel involved in the task, suggested improvements for better coordination between the Government, ministries and agencies, employers' and workers' organizations in monitoring and implementation.

To successfully and effectively achieve the above, there is need for more and continued technical assistance from the ILO, donors and other international agencies for training, setting up of data banks, review of existing situations and shortcomings and initiating new techniques and enquiries.

Finally, for the specific effects and implications of structural adjustment programmes on employment and manpower planning to be properly observed and handled early enough to avoid undesirable developments, the sectoral approach to manpower planning should be adopted instead of concentrating on nationwide and macro-manpower planning. The sectoral approach should be encouraged particularly with respect to different economic sectors and the public and private sectors.

References

Amjad, R. (ed). 1989. *Human resource planning: The Asian experience* (New Delhi, ILO/ARTEP).

Ashby, E. 1960. *Investment in education: The Report of the Commission on Post-School Certificate and Higher Education in Nigeria* (Lagos, Federal Ministry of Education).

Badada, U. 1986. *A study of new approaches, methods and techniques in generating, managing and utilizing labour market information* (Geneva, ILO).

Federal Republic of Nigeria Official Gazette (Lagos) Vol. 78, 31 May 1991.

ILO/JASPA. 1989a. *Wages, incomes policies and employment in Uganda* (Addis Ababa).

—. 1989b. *Guidelines and methodological approaches to human resources in Africa* (Addis Ababa).

—. 1990. *Alleviating unemployment and poverty under adjustment* (Addis Ababa).

Nigam, S.B.L. 1988a. *Labour market information programme in Zambia* (Addis Ababa).

—. 1988b. *Labour market information programmes and key informal systems in Africa and other developing countries* (Tripartite National Seminar on Labour Market Information, United Republic of Tanzania).

Psacharopoulos, G. and M. Woodham. 1985. *Education for development: An analysis of investment choices* (A World Bank Publication, Oxford University Press).

Raftopoulos, B. 1986. *New approaches, methods and techniques in generating, managing and utilizing labour market information in Zimbabwe* (Geneva, ILO).

Richter, L. 1989. *Upgrading labour market information in developing countries: Problems, progress and prospects* (Geneva, ILO).

Ukwu, U.I., et al. 1991. *Multi-Sectoral Needs Assessment Mission Report on Employment and Social Welfare* (Lagos, Federal Ministry of Finance and Economic Development and United Nations Development Programme).

6

Do continued skill shortages in Botswana imply that manpower planning has failed ?

Christopher Colclough*

1. Introduction

Botswana is one of the few countries in Africa which has practised man-power planning at the macro-level consistently over the past two decades. It provides a useful context, therefore, in which to assess the adequacy of manpower planning methods and assumptions, in comparison with subsequently revealed economic outcomes.

Manpower planners, in Botswana and elsewhere, have spent only a small proportion of their time and effort in preparing forecasts. The data they have gathered, and the analyses they have undertaken, have been used to address a wide range of policy questions which have probably made their endeavours separately useful and worthwhile. In this paper, however, we focus upon a narrow range of technical questions concerning the accuracy of their forecasts of future demand for skilled and educated workers in the formal sector of the economy. The fact is, as we shall demonstrate, that skill shortages in Botswana have, in some ways, become more intense over the period 1965-90. To what extent does this imply that manpower planning and, in particular, manpower forecasting has failed?

2. The enduring nature of Botswana skill shortages

The remarkable economic progress achieved in Botswana over its first two decades of independence is well known. Following the discovery and exploitation of diamonds and copper in the early 1970s, the economy expanded dramatically. Over the period 1965-88, Botswana's average annual per capita income growth rate was, at 8.6 per cent, considerably higher than any other of the 100 or so countries for which data are available.[1] In consequence the country moved from one of the 20 poorest countries to middle-income status over a very short period of time.

---

* Institute of Development Studies, Brighton, Sussex.

[1] Comparative growth rates of income per capita in the Asian newly industrializing countries and areas over the same period were Singapore, 7.2 per cent, the Republic of Korea, 6.8 per cent and Hong Kong 6.3 per cent (World Bank, 1990).

This growth in economic activity posed a great challenge for the country's educators. The country came to independence in 1966 with a post-primary education system which was, relative to the size of its population, one of the more underdeveloped in Africa. Only one government secondary school had been opened and that not until 1965. Thus, such secondary schooling opportunities as existed had been a product of missionary rather than government initiative, and all post-secondary education had to be pursued outside the country. There were therefore very few Batswana who had the benefit of higher education, and the economy was dependent upon expatriate workers in most of the jobs requiring the application of professional or technical skills.

As will be shown, Botswana's education system expanded very rapidly indeed in response to this unsatisfactory inheritance. But in spite of this, and of the large amounts of money and planning attention which have been directed to the problem of localization, the dependence upon foreign skills and expertise has remained strong.

Partly, and most obviously, this reflected economic success: formal employment expanded at almost nine per cent per year between 1964 and 1988 and a far higher proportion of the population benefited from wage and salary incomes, by the late 1980s, as a result (table 6.1). Some increase in the need for non-citizen skills, was, perhaps, an inevitable consequence of such rapid growth. Table 6.1, for example, shows that the sevenfold increase of employment between 1964 and 1988 was associated with a quadrupling of the number of expatriates employed in the country. This proved costly, in both economic and political terms. On the one hand, expatriate salaries and allowances sharply increased labour costs and added to foreign exchange outflows via remittances. Politically, it proved a source of resentment for many middle-level national workers seeking faster promotions and more autonomy for national staff. The Government, on the other hand, was able to claim that localization, in the sense of reducing relative dependence upon expatriates, was progressing: the proportion of non-citizen workers fell from nine per cent to about five per cent of total employment between 1964 and 1988 (table 6.1).

Nevertheless, the skill profile of formal employment also changed very substantially over the first two decades of independence. Even in 1972 the economy was still relatively simple, dominated as it was by the public sector, and comprising mainly commercial, transport and other service employment for primarily agrarian activities. The main focus of technical skills outside government was at that time the construction sector, which comprised a handful of large contracting companies, expatriate owned and staffed at all levels above semi-skilled. These had based themselves in Botswana initially in connection with the building of the new capital city, Gaborone, in the mid-1960s. By the early 1970s they were looking forward to, but only just beginning to profit from, a large number of contracts to build the mining and urban infrastructure which the then recent discoveries of copper, nickel and diamonds had facilitated. Over the following 15 years, the economy became much more complex and diversified. Two sectors which had hardly existed before – mining and, to a lesser extent, manufacturing – became major users of skilled technical personnel. Similarly the technical departments of government expanded sharply, reflecting the increased need for negotiation, management and inspection of large-scale, highly sophisticated

Table 6.1. Botswana, formal sector employment and population, 1964-88 ('000s)

Sector/status	1964[1]	1972	1986	1988
Public sector:[2]				
Citizen		12.4	51.0	56.2
Non-citizen		1.1	1.4	1.5
Total		13.6	52.4	57.2
Non-citizen (per cent)		8.5	2.7	2.6
Private & parastal sectors:				
Citizen		24.2	73.3	106.2
Non-citizen		2.3	5.2	7.1
Total		26.5	78.5	113.3
Non-citizen (per cent)		8.6	6.6	6.3
Total:				
Citizen	20.5	36.6	124.3	162.4
Non-citizen	2.1	3.4	6.6	8.6
Total	22.6	40.1	130.9	171.0
Non-citizen (per cent)	9.2	8.5	5.1[3]	5.0
Population	503.0	585.0	1 128.0	1 211.1
Employment as per cent of population	4.5	6.8	11.6	14.1
Average annual growth of employment 1964-88 (per cent)				8.8

[1] Sectoral detail not available on same basis as for later years. [2] Defined as central and local government including all education sector employees. [3] Estimates of 3,867 and 5,696 shown in Employment Survey Reports for 1986 and 1988 have been increased by 1,350 and 1,440 respectively to allow for expatriate workers in the private sector who were self-employed. Workers in the latter category were not covered by the annual employment surveys after 1973. Total employment for 1986 shown above thus omits Batswana self-employed persons in the private sector.

Source: Colclough and McCarthy, 1980, tables 7.3 and 8.2; Republic of Botswana, 1973, table 2.1; Republic of Botswana, 1987a, table 1; Republic of Botswana, 1987b, table 2; Central Statistical Office, Gaborone, Work permit records; Republic of Botswana, 1989 (*Labour Statistics 1988*).

projects, upon which the growing fortunes of the Government and, more indirectly, the people of Botswana, strongly depended.

The changes which this brought for the educational structure of the formal sector labour force are summarized in table 6.2. It shows that there was a marked improvement in the educational background of citizen workers between 1972 and 1986. Those who had had no secondary schooling were reduced from around 90 per cent of the total to about two-thirds over those years. Furthermore, those with five years of secondary schooling or more had risen from negligible proportions to about 12 per cent of citizen employment. When one recalls the rapidity of citizen employment growth (from 36,000 to over 124,000 workers over this period, as shown in table 6.1), these proportional changes indicate substantial progress with upgrading the formal qualifications of the citizen labour force.

Surprisingly, however, the educational structure of non-citizen employment changed even more markedly. The number of non-citizens holding degrees quadru-

Table 6.2. Botswana, educational background of formal sector workers by citizenship, 1972 and 1986 (per cent)

Educational level	1972			1986		
	Citizen	Non-citizen	Total	Citizen	Non-citizen	Total
No schooling/ primary only	88.6	39.7	84.5	66.9	11.1	64.6
Forms 1 or 2	3.1	4.0	3.2	3.0	1.7	2.9
Forms 3 or 4	5.7	15.7	6.5	18.3	5.8	17.8
Form 5	2.1	19.8	3.6	7.1	13.6	7.4
Diploma/certificate/ "A" level	0.1	5.1	0.5	2.7	26.3	3.7
Degree	0.4	16.0	1.7	2.0	41.5	3.7
Total	100.0	100.0	100.0	100.0	100.0	100.0

Source: Republic of Botswana 1973, Table B7, p.131, and special tabulation of results from the 1986 Employment Survey, provided by the Government Statistician, Gaborone.

pled – from 550 to 2,100 – and, as table 6.2 shows, their proportional importance increased from 16 to more than 40 per cent of all non-citizens employed. Equally, those with some education beyond Form 5 increased from one-fifth to more than two-thirds of all non-citizens employed, with a concomitant sharp reduction in the proportion having little or no formal schooling. It is clear, then, that the expatriates employed in Botswana were by the late 1980s a much more educated group than their equivalents had been shortly after the country's independence.

It is, of course, possible that this increase in the educational qualifications of non-citizen employees mainly reflected the general upgrading of educational access and standards in northern countries which occurred over this period – or, alternatively, increased competition amongst non-citizens seeking to work in Botswana – rather than a change in the technical or managerial responsibilities associated with the jobs open to them. There is, however, a range of evidence which suggests that this interpretation would not be correct. Firstly, there was a real increase in the levels of education and training required by employers of citizens hired into jobs previously held by expatriates. For example, the proportion of jobs held by non-citizens which were said by employers to require less than three years of secondary schooling, if the present incumbents were to be replaced by nationals, was reduced from around half to less than 10 per cent of the total between 1972 and 1984. Equally, sharp increases in the proportions requiring higher education were reported (see table 6.13, below, and accompanying text discussion). Thus, the increased educational qualifications of expatriates working in Botswana were at least partly a function of changes in national hiring standards for the jobs in question rather than merely of the increased availability of more highly qualified people from abroad.

Secondly, survey evidence indicates that expatriates became increasingly concentrated in the more skilled or responsible jobs in the economy over the two decades following independence. Table 6.3 summarizes some of this evidence. It should be noted that whilst the data for 1972 cover all expatriate employment, those for 1986 exclude the self-employed. Those, comprising around 1,350 persons, were

Table 6.3. Botswana, occupational distribution of expatriate employment, 1972 and 1986

Occupational group	1972		1986[1]	
	Number	Per cent	Number	Per cent
Professional and technical workers, of which:	1 071	44.8	3 041	59.7
Engineers, architects, surveyors	110	4.6	472	9.3
Engineering technicians	95	4.0	571	11.2
Nurses and midwives	55	2.3	145	2.8
Accountants, economists, etc.	103	4.3	353	6.9
Secondary & higher education teachers	217	9.1	780	15.3
Primary teachers	229	9.6	215	4.2
Other teachers	63	2.6	167	3.3
Other professional and technical	199	8.3	338	6.6
Managerial workers	386	16.1	939	18.4
Clerical, sales and service workers	462	19.3	318	6.2
Production workers, of which:	472	19.7	796	15.6
Foremen	144	6.0	160	3.1
Fitters	62	2.6	364	7.1
Other production	266	11.1	272	5.3
Total	2 391	100.0	5 094	100.0

[1] Data for 1986 omit approximately 1,350 self-employed expatriates in the private sector for whom no occupational details were available.

Source: Calculated from Ministry of Finance and Development Planning, 1973: *Manpower and employment in Botswana*, Table 8.6, pp. 117-120; and from Central Statistical Office: *Employment Survey, 1986*.

mainly in the professional/technical or managerial groupings. Thus, both the number and proportion of expatriates at the upper end of the occupational hierarchy are underestimated in the table.

Notwithstanding these important omissions, the data still indicate a strong shift in the composition of expatriate employment towards technical and professional jobs, with the proportion in this group increasing from 45 to 60 per cent over the period. A particular increase in the dependence upon expatriate engineers, surveyors and related technicians is evident: this group, comprising less than 9 per cent of expatriate employment in 1972, accounted for more than one-fifth of the total by the mid-1980s, following a fivefold increase in their numbers over the intervening years. Other occupations where dependence upon non-citizen skills continued to increase were accountants, and teachers in secondary and higher education, which together accounted for a further fifth of expatriate employment by 1986.

Lower down the occupational hierarchy, on the other hand, the localization progress was rapid. This was particularly so amongst clerical, sales and service workers, which accounted for only 6 per cent of expatriates employed in 1986 (down from almost 20 per cent). The proportion of non-citizen production workers was also much reduced, with the single exception of skilled electrical and mechanical fitters, where the growth in demand continued to outstrip that of suitably qualified Batswana, and where the number of non-citizen workers increased sixfold over the period shown.

Table 6.4. Botswana, employees holding work permits (private and parastatal sectors only) in December 1986, by subject of degree or diploma

Subject area	Degree		Diploma	
	Number	Per cent	Number	Per cent
General	2	0.2	9	0.5
Teaching	41	4.9	140	8.4
Fine arts	22	2.7	17	1.0
Humanities	19	2.3	13	0.8
Religion	1	0.1	2	0.1
Social sciences	54	6.5	34	2.0
Commerce, etc.	166	20.0	263	15.7
Law	15	1.8	4	0.2
Natural sciences	106	12.8	56	3.3
Maths/computing	48	5.8	36	2.1
Health	42	5.1	47	2.8
Construction	18	2.2	141	8.4
Other trades	26	3.1	340	20.4
Engineering	217	26.1	430	25.7
Home economics	15	1.8	15	0.9
Agriculture	12	1.4	21	1.3
Transport and communications	4	0.5	33	2.0
Service trades	8	1.0	42	2.5
Mass communications	8	1.0	13	0.8
Other	6	0.7	19	1.1
Total	830	100.0	1 675	100.0

Source: Special tabulation of data from work permit records.

Reflecting these changes in the occupational structure of expatriate employment, so too the qualifications held by those employed became markedly more technical in nature over the period. The detailed qualifications of those working in the public sector are not known. However, a study of work permit records for December 1986 revealed that of 830 expatriate workers with degrees in the private and parastatal sectors, one-quarter had graduated in engineering, and a further fifth in each of maths/natural sciences and accounting/commercial studies. Those with diplomas had also specialized heavily in engineering or commercial subjects (table 6.4).

The age and experience structure of expatriate employment have also changed in ways which are consistent with the above picture. The median age of non-citizen workers appears to have changed little between 1972 and the mid-1980s: as indicated by table 6.5, exactly the same proportion of expatriate workers (43 per cent) were aged less than 36 years in those two years. There were other changes of importance, however: first, the proportion of very young employees (9.2 per cent in 1972) was halved by 1986; second, one-third of the total employees were bunched in the mid-career age-range (36-45 years) in the mid-1980s compared with only one-quarter in the early 1970s. Thus, the age distribution has been narrowed, in ways which are consistent with the increased concentration upon technical expertise. Com-

Table 6.5. Botswana, age distribution of expatriate workers, 1972 and 1986

Age group	1972		1986	
	Simple	Cumulative	Simple	Cumulative
16-25	9.2	9.2	4.7	4.7
26-35	33.6	42.8	38.0	42.7
36-45	26.4	69.2	33.8	76.5
46-55	20.5	89.7	16.2	92.7
56-65	7.8	97.6	6.4	99.1
66+	2.1	99.7	0.7	99.8
Total	100.0	100.0	100.0	100.0

Note: 1972 data refer to all non-citizen workers; 1986 data to work permit holders only.

Sources: Ministry of Finance and Development Planning, 1973: *Manpower and employment in Botswana*, table B18, p. 146, and from work permit records for 1986.

Table 6.6. Botswana, years of previous job experience of expatriate employees with work permits in the private and parastatal sectors, December 1986

Years of experience	Number	Relative frequency	Cumulative frequency
None	48	1.2	1.2
1-5	491	12.0	13.2
6-10	861	21.1	34.3
11-15	804	19.7	54.0
16-20	614	15.0	69.1
20+	815	20.0	89.0
Not known	448	11.0	100.0
Total	4 081	100.0	–

Source: Work permit records

parative data on the prior levels of job-experience of non-citizen employees are not available in detailed form for 1972.

However, rough calculations based upon the 1972 survey suggest that the proportion of highly experienced expatriates in post was substantially less than the 46 per cent who were reported to have over 15 years of prior job experience in 1986 (table 6.6). In all of the above ways the average skill levels of non-citizens working in Botswana appear to have risen considerably since the early 1970s, and have become quite strongly concentrated in a limited number of occupations and areas of expertise. These circumstances indicate the existence of a pronounced excess demand in Botswana for a range of maths/science-based technical and commercial skills.[2]

[2] It is usually best, in economics, to explore the nature of skill shortages by using some index of relative wage movements for different categories of occupation or skill. In Botswana, and in some other ex-colonial countries, this is difficult, firstly because wage differentials at independence were extremely wide, and reflected the much higher wages paid to whites compared with blacks, and secondly because the subsequent evolution of differentials throughout the economy was heavily influenced by the administered, rather than competitively determined, pay scales of the civil service. Tracking the movement of differentials over time, in such economies, does not necessarily provide adequate proxy evidence for changes in the relative demand for different skills.

Thus, the localization problem, though proportionately smaller, will be more difficult to solve during the 1990s than in the early years of independence, when many expatriates were still occupying posts at middle levels of the occupational hierarchy. Indeed, in some technical occupations – most notably engineering and related jobs – the localization task increased in both absolute and relative terms over the twenty-five years following independence.

In what follows we examine some of the reasons for the tightening of the skill shortage in Botswana, paying particular attention to the ways in which the provision of education and training facilities were planned.

3. Was planning to blame?

As nationalist pressures for independence spread throughout Africa in the late 1950s and early 1960s, and as political freedom was gained by even the smallest and poorest States, the preoccupation of colonial administrations with minimizing territorial expenditures began to be replaced by a new concern to accelerate domestic development and to allocate as effectively as possible the aid monies which would be made available to the new governments. In Africa, where education throughout the continent had mainly been left to missionary activities or to local endeavour, and where, as a result, very small proportions of the population had had access to any form of post-primary schooling, it appeared obvious that one of the greatest priorities for early public investment should be the education sector. The "manpower constraint" was viewed to be critical everywhere in Africa – a view which was given strong intuitive plausibility by the high proportion of expatriates occupying the senior jobs in the fledgling private sectors and in the state administrations throughout the continent. In most countries, however, the scale of obvious educational needs would continue to dwarf the resources available. In response, manpower planning, which attempted to relate the structure and dimensions of the formal education and training system to the anticipated demands of employers for educated and trained workers, was increasingly advocated as an appropriate planning instrument to help establish policy priorities.

From the above perspective, Botswana's circumstances were classic within Africa. Colonial neglect, extreme poverty, a largely uneducated population, high dependence upon expatriate skills, and the presence of significant mineral resources which held out a possibility of rapid economic growth together implied that, implicitly or explicitly, some form of manpower forecasting would be used to provide a framework for educational investment. How then should Botswana's subsequent experience be interpreted? Should the continuing skill shortages documented above be taken to imply a failure of planning? Or should the formidable progress made in expanding the education and training system over intervening years be judged to be a great success, in comparison with which skill shortages are unimportant – worrying to economists, perhaps, but not to the increasingly prosperous population of Botswana at large? These are the main questions which inform our assessments of planning experience and outcomes which now follow.

Early planning initiatives

In spite of the complete absence of any publicly financed post-primary education facilities, and of the major deficiencies in coverage and quality of primary schooling over the eleven years 1955-65, more than 18 per cent of the colonial government's development expenditure had been spent on education,[3] and in 1965 – the year before independence – it accounted for more than 20 per cent of the recurrent budget. Thus, the continued deficiencies within education were a symptom of more general fiscal stringency; in view of the pressing needs in all sectors at that time, education had not been neglected much more than anything else. Moreover, given the extreme poverty of the country at independence, it was obvious that the government would need to assess its development priorities carefully – not only as between education and other sectors, but also within the education sector itself.

A British Economic Survey mission, which visited the territory immediately prior to independence to assess development prospects, was influential in shaping the early framework for development policy. Its report was clear as to where the priorities in education should lie: "our investigation is concerned primarily with the creation in the shortest possible time, with such financial means as may be available, of a stock of trained local manpower capable of serving the country's political and economic growth" (Republic of Botswana, 1966a:71). Although the report expressed deep concern over conditions in primary education, it saw the more urgent priority as being the expansion of the higher levels of the system. It recommended ways of using resources in the primary system more effectively, but these were essentially cost-saving measures, and the authors of the report felt that "no increase in Government recurrent expenditure on primary education ... can be expected in the near future" (ibid:73).

Foremost in the minds of the survey team was how to achieve development in a way which did not significantly boost the Government's budget deficit in the short term, but which, in the medium term, secured a growing domestic revenue which would reduce the country's dependence upon grants-in-aid from the British Government. Though mineral deposits were known to be substantial, the team considered that their development would be gradual, and would have effects upon revenue only in the long-term. Thus, for the foreseeable future, agriculture was expected to be the basis of the economy, and the recurrent budget deficit would remain for many years. There was a strong emphasis upon the need for stringent economic and financial management, reflecting a highly pessimistic view of the prospects for economic growth.

Accordingly, initial expectations were that there would exist neither the need nor the ability to increase the size of public sector employment in Botswana, and the emphasis of British advice in the education sector was to focus upon post-primary expansion so as to tackle a large, but essentially static, localization task. The report anticipated that the public service would grow by less than 5 per cent over the period 1965-70, and that the private and parastatal sectors would have negligible

---

[3] See Republic of Botswana, 1966a: Appendix II.

growth requirements with less than 100 new jobs requiring middle secondary schooling or above being expected between 1965 and 1970.[4] Essentially, then, the main need was to localize existing posts, and, since the private sector was too small to merit attention, growth requirements were expected to be very small indeed. It was suggested that enrolments in the first form at secondary schools should increase from 600 in 1965 to 770 in 1970,[5] by which time the secondary system was expected to have sufficient capacity to service the country's longer-term requirements for educated personnel.

Although the new Government of Botswana rejected the conservatism of some aspects of the report of the British team, its priorities for the education sector were accepted. In the Transitional Development Plan (Republic of Botswana, 1966b), the Government committed no new funds to primary education, and adopted the Ministry of Overseas Development projections for secondary school developments.[6] As can be seen from Table 6.7, enrolments in Form I were planned to increase from 770 to 775 only, between 1970 and 1975. There was to be a significant increase in provision for teacher training, and higher education together with technical training were to be expanded, though by how much remained unclear. These elements had also been proposals of the British team.

It took two years for the Government to realize that Botswana's needs for workers with post-primary education or training were likely to be substantially greater than had been envisaged by the Economic Survey Mission. Between 1965 and 1967, enrolments in Form I had risen only from 601 to 633 students. But in the first National Development Plan, published in the following year, projections for secondary school placements in 1975 rose from the 775 cited earlier to 1,700 (Republic of Botswana, 1968). The mining complex proposed for Selebi-Pikwe now appeared viable for the near future, and the infrastructure requirements of this project would be likely to boost significantly the demands for skilled and educated workers of all kinds. The revised enrolment projections in the plan were based upon crude manpower estimates, linked to a fairly rapid rate of economic growth which was now more confidently expected in the light of the good prospects for minerals development. Though there was a dearth of information concerning the underlying trends in the economy, and no employment figures other than those revealed by a population census which had been held four years earlier, it remained a praxis of development policy that post-primary educational development would be undertaken only insofar as this could be justified by manpower forecasts. These, from the perspective of labour absorption, became increasingly optimistic, and the publication of the first Plan marked the beginning of a period of very rapid secondary school expansion. The number of placements in secondary schools doubled between 1967 and 1969, and they were to double again by 1973. The Transitional Plan's 1975 target was overtaken in 1968, and that of the first Plan was also to be exceeded several years before the target date.

In the second Plan (Republic of Botswana, 1970), a slightly more sophisticated approach to the problem of manpower forecasting was used. In this case sec-

---

[4] See Republic of Botswana, 1966a.

[5] The majority of pupils were to be enrolled in non-government secondary schools.

[6] See Republic of Botswana, 1966b.

Table 6.7. Botswana, planned and actual enrolments in government and aided secondary schools

	Form 1	Form 4	Total
Actual enrolments			
1965	601	84	1 307
1970	1 336	292	3 905
1975	2 812	891	8 434
1980	3 929	1 557	13 424
1985	5 416	2 170	20 099
1990			
Planned 1970			
ODA Economic Survey Mission	770	230	2 470
Planned 1975			
Transitional Plan (1966)	775	360	2 970
NDP 1 (1968)	1 700	609	5 651
NDP 2 (1970)	2 760	861	8 649
NDP 3 (1973)	2 765	865	8 483

Source: Central Statistics Office: *Education Statistics 1988*, and documents cited in table.

toral employment totals generated by an employment survey held in 1967 were projected forward assuming a rate of economic growth of 8 per cent per year. Occupational forecasts covering the ten-year period to 1980 were based on the occupational structure of Zambia revealed by a detailed survey which had been held in that country in 1965.[7] The most notable result of these projections, based as they were on some imaginative assumptions, was that earlier demand estimates for educated workers were again revised upwards considerably. The new projected Form I enrolments for 1975 were put at 2,760 students — more than five times as great as Form I enrolments had been in 1966, and more than three-and-a-half times as great as had been planned for 1975 by the Transitional Plan which had been published at the time of independence.

But doubts about the wisdom of this accelerating expansion programme were beginning to be raised. The donors who were financing the capital development of the education sector[8] felt that there might be difficulty in absorbing the proposed numbers of secondary school graduates: mining development was expected to be highly capital intensive, and its impact on the rate of economic growth was expected to be much more significant than upon the rate of job-creation. Although the Second Plan allocated more than 80 per cent of development expenditure in education to the secondary schools and the university,[9] Botswana's aid donors began to feel that there

[7] See Republic of Zambia, 1966.

[8] The United Kingdom provided most of the aid to education (as to other sectors at that time). However, the United States of America, Canada and Sweden were also sources of bilateral support to education.

[9] Details can be found in Republic of Botswana, 1970.

were other pressing priorities which perhaps deserved more attention; conditions in rural primary schools, for example, were still especially bad, and improvements since independence had depended upon self-help activities and the limited fund-raising capacity of District Councils. Moreover, with regard to the post-primary sector, it was unclear whether the proposed balance between general and technical education was appropriate. Although limited attempts had been made to anticipate requirements for school-leavers and university graduates, there was considerable uncertainty concerning the amount of provision needed for artisan, technical and commercial training. Thus, the donors (and, amongst them, particularly the British) suggested that, as part of the lead up to the Third Plan, further expansion of the post-primary system for the period 1973-78 should be justified by a detailed study of the manpower situation in the country. The Government accepted the need for such a survey: the rapid economic progress made by Botswana since independence had already considerably enhanced the country's needs for skilled workers of all kinds. The growth in demand had far outstripped the capacity of the education system to produce educated and trained persons, and, as documented earlier in this chapter, the initial shortages of local manpower, and the consequent number of non-citizens who had to be recruited, grew rapidly. Progress with localization became an increasingly sensitive political issue, and urgent measures to reduce the nation's dependence upon expatriate labour were judged necessary.

The shift to purposive manpower planning

These pressures led the Government in 1971 to commission, using British development loan funds, a national manpower survey covering all sectors of the economy. This survey, which was a personal, rather than a postal, enumeration, covered all establishments and government organizations in the formal sector. Within each establishment, data were obtained on total employment and wages paid, by sex and citizenship, and on a wide range of personal and occupational characteristics of each skilled worker.[10] In addition, data were collected on the education and training requirements for entry into each skilled job (including vacancies) as defined by the employer.[11] The resulting report (Ministry of Finance and Development Planning, 1973) represented the country's first comprehensive approach to manpower planning. The main aim of the survey had been to obtain a detailed description of the occupational structure and of the skilled labour force. It generated a series of matrices for 10 economic sectors and 17 departments of central government, showing skilled employment and vacancies in 1972, cross-classified by citizenship, 40 occupations and eight levels of "required" education. These matrices formed the basis for projections of future levels of demand for skilled workers. They were incorporated in

---

[10] A skilled worker was defined as an employed person holding, or doing a job which in the employer's view would then require some post-primary formal education or training. This, quite deliberately, provided a fairly generous definition of skilled employment. It emerged that one-third of those in formal employment were "skilled", according to this definition.

[11] In the case of the public service, these data were obtained from schemes-of-service or, in some cases, from departmental heads.

the Third Development Plan (1973-78), and the agreed expansion programme for the education and training sectors was derived from its results. Its projections were revised and incorporated in the Fourth Plan covering the period 1976-81 – and it continued to provide guidelines for the formulation, particularly, of the quantitative aspects of educational policy for some years. The related data covering total employment in the formal sector, progress made with localization and the structure of wages and salaries also proved to be extremely useful for policy purposes in a number of different ways.[12]

As regards the institutional structure for planning, a number of committees were established in the early 1970s which provided a forum where important aspects of human resources policy could be resolved. These included a National Employment, Manpower and Incomes Council, a Wages Policy Committee, and an Education Advisory Committee. Each of these were interministerial bodies, with advisory status to the relevant minister. Their secretariat was provided by the Division of Economic Affairs within the Ministry of Finance and Development Planning, usually in the person of one of the planning officers responsible for human resources policy. These institutional arrangements were consolidated in 1980, when an Employment Policy Unit (EPU) was established within the macroeconomic Section of the Division of Economic Affairs. This unit was headed by an Employment Coordinator and included three other planning officers. Its main responsibility was to help translate the Government's concern for employment creation into effective action. Its modes of work were primarily analytic and advisory – its advice being adopted and implemented via a series of committees (including some of those mentioned above) for which EPU provided the secretariat, or on which it was represented. In addition, it was given responsibility for implementing and monitoring a new Financial Assistance Policy which provided wage subsidies to new or expanding enterprises in the private sector, under carefully defined circumstances, as a direct means of supporting employment creation. Also amongst its responsibilities fell manpower planning, and one of its officers was given primary responsibility for this area of work.

These latter institutional arrangements represented a considerable increase in the resources available for work on human resources planning in comparison with the earlier, more ad hoc, procedures. Five manpower planning reports were produced for each of the years 1982-85 and 1987, which attempted to provide detailed manpower forecasts to the end of the century, in order to give information which could be a guide for the planning of education and training, and for overseas recruitment. The reports, using data collected by the annual employment surveys, and incorporating information derived from a wide range of other sources, provided detailed estimates of future employment (usually classified by economic sector, occupation and levels of required education and training). These estimates were compared with expected outflows of students from the education and training systems, and future expected manpower "imbalances" were derived.

These analyses were gallant attempts to integrate all of the information available on trends in the formal labour market, and to derive conclusions for educa-

---

[12] These are outlined and discussed in Colclough, 1976.

tional policies from detailed projections of labour demand classified by occupation and levels of "required" education. As such, they were vulnerable to the full range of objections which such enquiries conventionally attract. In addition, however, there were other problems relating particularly to the database used for planning, and to the technical assumptions used by the planners which provided separate and significant sources of bias. As will be demonstrated below, these appear to have affected both the quantitative aspects of this planning work, and, thus, the nature of the conclusions derived for educational policy.

How accurate were the assumptions used by the planners?

Unlike the 1973 study, which had the advantage of a good data base provided by the national manpower survey, the preparation of manpower projections in Botswana over the 1980s was seriously hampered by a lack of reliable data. Planners had to rely upon the annual employment survey, which was a postal enumeration targeted at owners of a sample of all licensed business establishments together with all local authorities and parastatal organizations. Central government departments were not always included. The methods and scope of the annual surveys meant that fairly high sampling errors were associated with their results. Equally, as is often the case with postal surveys, the detailed information classifying employment by occupation and some other variables was often particularly unreliable.

Notwithstanding these difficulties, the earliest employment surveys date back to the early 1970s and they thus provide a source of time-series information which can be used to test the efficacy of some of the critical assumptions used in plan preparation. Those which most strongly affect the validity and accuracy of manpower projections are the following three:

(i) the assumptions made concerning the future rate of growth of sectoral output;

(ii) the elasticities linking the growth of sectoral output to the growth of sectoral employment;

(iii) the coefficients linking the growth of sectoral employment to the growth of demand for labour with different skill and occupational characteristics.

In what follows, an attempt will be made to establish some empirical basis for these relationships in Botswana – thereby to assess the extent to which the manpower planning documents adopted assumptions which are empirically defensible.

(i) *Economic growth:* In an economy where the two main productive sectors have been influenced primarily by the weather and by minerals discoveries, – particularly diamonds – one would expect the forecasting record to be less accurate than in economies less subject to variations beyond human control. Nevertheless the record with economic forecasting in Botswana has not been at all bad. Table 6.8 shows the recent growth experience, by sector, and compares this with the projections of recent development plans.

Table 6.8 shows the medium-term (five-year) projections for GDP given in the Third and Fifth Development Plans, and compares these with reported outcomes. They demonstrate that at least during most of the period under review, the

Table 6.8.   Botswana, gross domestic product: A comparison of actual and projected outcomes (millions of pula, at 1979/80 prices)

Economic sector	GDP 1979/80	GDP 1984/5	Growth 1979/80-1984/5 (per cent p.a.)	NDP V projected growth 1979/80-1984/5 (per cent p.a.)	GDP 1985/6	Growth 1984/5-1985/6 (per cent p.a.)	NDP VI projected growth 1985/6-1990/1 (per cent p.a.)
Agriculture	83.3	48.0	-10.4	7.3	48.0	–	6.5
Mining & quarrying	210.7	560.6	21.6	15.8	673.2	20.1	3.5
Manufacturing	29.2	46.0	9.5	10.2	45.0	-2.2	8.3
Electricity and water	15.0	19.6	5.5	8.2	20.7	5.6	7.2
Construction	36.4	32.3	-2.4	-5.2	30.3	-6.2	3.5
Wholesale and retail	157.0	204.4	5.4	6.8	223.4	9.3	3.8
Transport and communications	13.6	25.2	13.1	6.5	26.1	3.6	5.0
Financial institutions	57.6	67.9	3.3	7.7	74.0	8.9	5.4
Household, social and community services	20.9	34.9	10.8	7.7	35.5	1.7	5.4
Government	92.6	156.2	11.0	11.4	165.7	6.1	5.1
Dummy sector	-14.8	-24.2	...	...	-26.3	...	...
Total	701.5	1170.9	10.8	10.1	1315.6	12.4	4.8
Total (excl. mining)	409.8	610.3	4.5	7.0	642.4	5.3	5.3

... = not applicable.

Source: GDP actuals: Central Statistics Office: *Statistical Bulletin*, March 1987, Vol. 12, No. 1, table 5B; Ministry of Finance and Development Planning, NDP V projections: *National Development Plan 1985-91*, December 1985, table 2.5; NDP VI projections, tables 2.10 and A.2.1.

overall rate of growth forecast by the planners was closely accurate. There was, however, less accuracy at the sectoral level. In general, the performance of the agricultural sector has been consistently overestimated during the 1970s and 1980s, and the remarkable contribution of mining has been underestimated. Notwithstanding these trends, the planners correctly forecast that the Botswana economy would enjoy remarkably high rates of growth over the periods shown. Moreover, the impact of the variation in sectoral growth rates – planned versus actual – for the extractive sectors is far less serious for employment planning than similar variations elsewhere in the economy, as will be seen below.

There is, however, a natural and healthy tendency in Botswana's planning documents to be more cautious about growth prospects over the longer term. Thus, for example, the 1973 manpower plan based its long-term projections from 1978-88 upon an overall real growth rate of GDP of around 6 per cent over those years. This compares with the average annual rate of around 12 per cent which was actually achieved. As a result, the long-term manpower projections of that plan were much greater underestimates – from this source alone – than the medium-term projections to 1978, which emerged as closely accurate.

By 1979/80 the planners had revised upwards their estimates for the 1980s, and expected an average rate of growth over the following five years of around 10 per cent. It can be seen from the table that this was almost exactly achieved, even though the average figure concealed strong sectoral variation. In particular, the poor performance by agriculture was largely responsible for the overestimation of growth outside the minerals sector in NDP V (actual growth of 4.5 per cent per annum compared with 7.0 per cent per annum projected – see table 6.8). If the drought had ended, and if agriculture had recovered, as had been expected, non-mining output growth would have been very close to the levels forecast for the five-year period.

It appears that this good medium-term forecasting record was not maintained, however, in NDP VI. Output growth was forecast to increase by less than five per cent annually over the period 1985/86-1990/91, compared with the continued average annual growth of around 12 per cent in real terms which now seems to have been maintained over those years. (Ministry of Finance and Development Planning, 1990, National Development Plan). This will therefore have been a source of forecasting error for employment projections prepared in the mid-1980s, to the extent that these were linked to rates of output growth expected at that time.

(ii) *Employment/output elasticities:* During the 1980s, manpower plans in Botswana adopted high employment/output elasticities. In most sectors these were assumed to take a value of unity – implying that a given proportionate increase in output would be associated with an increase in employment by the same proportionate amount. This assumption is unusual, and controversial, in that it implies that the average productivity of labour will remain constant, rather than increase over time, as would usually be expected to happen. By contrast the 1973 manpower plan had adopted an overall employment elasticity of 0.64,[13] allowing for moderate productivity growth over the following five years.

---

[13] This aggregate estimate, however, was an average derived from different assumptions made for each economic sector (Ministry of Finance and Development Planning, 1973: Appendix F).

Table 6.9 assembles information relevant to testing these assumptions in the face of experience since the mid-1970s. The table shows sectoral output estimates, in constant prices, for the years 1976/77, 1980/81 and 1985/86, and employment estimates for the same years. Comparison of the revealed average rates of growth of output and of employment over the period allows a test of the accuracy of the elasticity assumptions made for those years. Actual elasticities are shown in table 6.10. These have been calculated without taking account of movements in real prices over the period and, in particular, the prices of labour and capital. Strictly, therefore, their use for projection purposes would involve the assumption that past trends in such prices would continue in the future. If the government were to have taken a more interventionist stance on incomes policy than it had since the early 1970s such assumptions would have been inappropriate. However, no major shift in distributional policies occurred over the period,[14] and, in these circumstances, elasticity estimates gross of price changes are best. They are interesting particularly from the points of view of their size and their stability.

As indicated above, in principle employment/output elasticities can be expected to be less than unity. Owing to technical progress, labour productivity tends to increase over time, leading to coefficients with a value of less than one. At first sight this appears from table 6.10 to be true in Botswana, with employment having increased at about half the rate of output growth between 1976 and 1985. That result, however, was heavily influenced by conditions in the mining sector. There, output can be increased markedly with little if any impact upon labour use. It can be seen that this was particularly so between 1980 and 1985, when output increased at a rate which was about 70 times greater than that of the growth of employment in the sector. Because of the proportional importance of diamonds output to total GDP, the elasticity relationship in mining strongly influenced that for the whole economy.

Outside mining, however, relationships between employment and output appear to have been rather different. Taking the non-mining economy as a whole, employment growth was exceeded by output growth by only about 6 per cent over the period 1976-85. This, of course, implies that real output per worker outside mining remained roughly constant over those years.

Although it is not entirely clear why this occurred, inspection of the size of the sectoral elasticities provides some clues. Of particular note are the very large elasticity estimates for manufacturing and construction, of 3.1 and 2.25 respectively. These estimates are high enough to imply the occurrence of quite sharp structural change in the type of activities, or firms, comprising these sectors. In manufacturing, part of the variability in labour-output ratios is explained by the importance of the Botswana Meat Commission in the sector's output. The years of drought were associated with quite sharp increases in cattle throughout, without concomitant increases in labour employed. In addition, however, it appears that in both manufacturing and construction there were marked shifts towards smaller, and often locally-owned establishments. If this is true, there will probably have been a change in production techniques towards those which use more labour per unit of capital than used to be

[14] Indeed the results of the Presidential Commission to Review Incomes Policy, 1990, imply, even now, considerably less intervention than was intended (albeit not achieved) in the past.

Table 6.9. Botswana, output and employment in the formal sector, 1976/77-1985/86

Economic sector	Gross domestic product, millions of pula at 1979/80 prices			Annual growth (per cent)			Formal sector employment (000's)			Annual growth (per cent)		
	1976/77	1980/81	1985/86[1]	1976-80	1980-85	1976-85	1976/77	1980/81	1985/86	1976/80	1980/85	1976/85
Freehold agriculture	8.0	6.2	2.7	-6.2	-15.3	-11.3	3.8	4.3	4.0	3.1	-1.4	0.6
Mining and quarrying	92.1	260.6	673.2	29.7	20.9	24.7	5.5	7.2	7.3	7.0	0.3	3.2
Manufacturing	34.6	37.0	45.0	1.7	4.0	3.0	4.5	5.6	10.1	5.1	12.5	9.3
Electricity and water	11.1	15.3	20.7	8.4	6.2	7.2	0.8	1.5	1.9	18.0	4.8	10.9
Construction	22.8	32.0	30.3	8.8	-1.1	3.2	6.2	12.4	11.6	21.2	-2.8	7.2
Wholesale and retail trade	81.4	163.8	223.4	19.1	6.4	11.9	10.9	10.4	18.3	-1.1	12.0	5.9
Transport and communications services	10.3	14.8	26.1	9.5	12.0	10.9	1.8	3.4	5.7	17.2	10.9	13.5
Financial institutions[2]	29.2	49.7	74.0	14.2	8.3	10.9	3.1	4.3	6.8	9.6	9.6	9.3
General government[2]	78.3	104.7	165.7	7.5	9.6	8.7	21.7	30.8	47.5	9.2	9.1	9.1
Household and other services	18.7	25.6	35.5	8.2	6.8	7.4	2.2	2.4	3.9	3.0	10.2	6.7
Total	378.6	693.0	1270.3	16.3	12.9	14.4	60.4	83.3	117.1	8.4	7.0	7.6
(excluding mining)	286.5	432.4	597.1	10.8	6.7	8.5	54.9	76.1	109.8	8.5	7.6	8.0

[1] Preliminary estimates. Traditional agricultural production is excluded from GDP. [2] The boundaries of the finance, government and other services sectors used for the GDP and the employment estimates do not exactly coincide.

Source: Central Statistics Office, National Accounts Statistics and Annual Employment Surveys.

Table 6.10. Botswana, calculation of employment/output elasticities[1]

Economic sector	Employment/output elasticities		
	1976-80	1980-85	1976-85
Mining & quarrying	0.24	0.01	0.13
Manufacturing	3.00	3.13	3.10
Electricity & water	2.14	0.77	1.51
Construction	2.41	–	2.25
Wholesale & retail trade	–	1.88	0.50
Transport & communications	1.81	0.91	1.24
Financial institutions	0.68	1.16	0.85
General government	1.23	0.95	1.05
Household & other services	0.37	1.50	0.91
Total	0.52	0.54	0.58
(excluding mining)	0.78	1.13	0.94

– = not available.

[1] Calculated by dividing the average annual growth of employment by the average annual growth in GDP from table 6.9. These estimates, therefore, are gross of changes in the real prices of labour and capital. See text for discussion of this issue.

the case. This, then, is to argue that the high employment elasticities in these sectors are more likely to have been a function of structural change than of any real fall in the productivity of labour.

Except in manufacturing, government and finance, the values of the employment elasticities have not been particularly stable – as attested by the comparison between the first and second halves of the period 1976-85. In the public sector, the elasticity appears to have been close to unity. This is as expected – the value of the output of government is basically the same as the size of the wage and salaries' bill. The latter will be determined by the size of the establishment and the unit cost of labour. Thus if wages and salaries are constant in real terms, unit costs will only rise as a result of incremental drift – which, in a still young civil service such as that in Botswana, is usually equivalent to between 1 and 3 per cent per year. Thus, a coefficient of close to unity is usual for the government sector. The fact that this was exceeded in Botswana was probably owing to the real salary declines which were achieved in the late 1970s, as compared to the period 1980-85.

Elsewhere, however, for those sectors where a comparison can be made, the coefficients appear to have been highly unstable – differing by a factor of 100 per cent or more as between the first and second halves of the period. The reasons for this will undoubtedly differ from sector to sector: in mining, the recruitment of sufficient workers to run the new diamond mine at Jwaneng was needed (almost) irrespective of the diamond production achieved there. Similar points can be made in the utilities sector. Thus, in a sequential sense, periods of overmanning followed by rapidly rising levels of labour productivity are to be expected. In other sectors, on the other hand, labour will be laid off or taken on more rapidly in response to changes in the demand conditions faced by the sector. The lessons of all this appear to be the following:

(a) The average (national) relationships between output and employment may appear to be stable, but in fact conceal very large differences in elasticities in different sectors of the economy.

(b) Elasticities have been high historically, and suggest that demand projections based upon unitary elasticities have been about right at least in some sectors. In others, however, the data suggest that even higher estimates would have been appropriate.

(c) The comparison between the late 1970s and early 1980s, however, suggests that one cannot necessarily expect stability in these coefficients over time. This is not only as between different sectors of the economy, but also *within* economic sectors over a ten-year period. In general the somewhat lower elasticities adopted in the 1973 report, in comparison with those of the 1980s, seem justifiable on the basis of this evidence.

Nevertheless, these results are not particularly promising from the point of view of economic forecasting. They do, at least, vindicate the fairly high elasticities assumed by Botswana's planners in the recent past – indeed in some sectors they demonstrate that even *those* assumptions have been, on balance, conservative in their implications for labour demand.

(iii) *Education and training coefficients:* Over a number of years one interesting characteristic of the employment surveys was to elicit information on the education and training background now required by employers of new recruits to each post in their firm. This information is available separately for each economic sector covered by the surveys. These data allow the calculation of sectoral education and training coefficients – which express the percentage of total employment in each sector in jobs "requiring" each level of education or training. It follows that if this "required" educational structure of sectoral employment is relatively stable over time, the coefficients can be applied to projected sectoral employment totals, to provide estimates of the required educational composition of future employment. This method was used for each of the manpower plans prepared between 1983-85, although a different approach was used in the 1973 Plan. It follows that variations between actual and projected outcomes arise from two sources: first, variations in the projected levels for total sectoral employment; second, variations in the sectoral education coefficients applied to these employment totals. Table 6.11 shows that the results of such variations have in fact had serious implications for successive manpower projections. The projected labour requirements for the whole economy in 2001 were put at 683,000 in 1983; they were revised downwards to 542,000 in 1984 and upwards again to 582,000 in 1985. The 1985 estimates, however, were still 15 per cent lower, in total, than those projected two years earlier. The impact of the revisions on projected demand for skilled and educated workers, however, was even stronger – with expected requirements for those with degrees or senior secondary education being halved as between 1983 and 1985. Such sharp changes in the projected demand for skills are greater than should reasonably be expected, and would, of course, have major implications for educational planning were their implications translated into the implied expansion programmes for education and training. Those who use these projections would be justified in concluding that the revisions which have occurred in

Table 6.11. Botswana, a comparison of demand projections, by level of education and training presented in successive manpower planning reports

Level of education and training	1983 report		1984 report		1985 report	
	1991	2001	1991	2001	1991	2001
Less than junior secondary	270 262	462 482	251 443	381 948	209 658	410 741
Less than junior secondary & training	40 188	82 438	29 551	48 105	40 609	65 933
Junior secondary	13 792	25 503	12 152	18 753	8 910	16 396
Senior secondary	6 506	11 886	5 720	8 043	3 556	5 854
Secondary & training	47 713	94 215	46 694	79 226	48 671	80 102
Degree or higher	3 721	6 867	3 681	5 913	2 194	3 458
Total	382 181	683 391	348 788	541 984	313 600	582 483

Note: Some categories of education and training in 1983 and 1984 have had to be combined, in order to allow comparison with 1985 report.

Sources: Ministry of Finance and Development Planning: *National Manpower Development Planning 1983*, table 4.3, p. 23; *National Manpower Development Planning 1984*, table 24, p. 38; *National Manpower Development Planning 1985*, table 22, p. 51.

successive manpower planning documents published during the 1980s are so great as to undermine their efficacy for purposes of educational planning.

Changes to the required education coefficients used in the projections have arisen mainly from changes in data availability as given by the employment surveys. The 1983 manpower plan used coefficients derived from the 1981 survey; those used for the 1984 plan were the five-year average of data from the surveys between 1979-83; and the 1985 plan used data generated by the 1984 survey. In each case estimates for central and local government were derived from analysis of schemes of service, and estimates for the informal and traditional agricultural sectors were included on the basis of information from the 1981 population census, the National Migration Study and from the Labour Force Survey.

The results of the projections for the economy as a whole are summarized and compared in table 6.12. This shows the proportion of total projected labour requirements in 2001, at each level of required education/training. It can be seen that the combined results of the changes in the coefficients led to particularly substantial differences in the expected proportion of jobs requiring degrees, and in the proportion requiring senior secondary schooling as between each of the plans. Overall, the latest projections shown imply a considerable reduction in the projected skill-intensity of the future labour force as compared with what had been projected two years before.[15] Quite apart from the issue of the different ways in which education coefficients were calculated in successive reports there is a separate set of questions concerning whether these coefficients can or should be treated as being stable over time for the purpose of making manpower projections. The recent manpower plans in

---

[15] There is evidence to suggest that this result was caused by ambiguities in the questionnaires, and/or by errors in coding the 1984 employment survey results. Some workers in jobs which were said to require degrees were misclassified as requiring training post-Form 5, resulting in an undercounting of degree-level requirements as compared with earlier years.

Table 6.12. Botswana, distribution of jobs by level of required education/training: Projected outcomes for 2001, as given by annual manpower reports (per cent)

	Year of plan		
	1983	1984	1985
Less than junior certificate (JC)	67.7	70.5	70.5
Less than JC plus training	12.1	8.9	11.3
Junior certificate	3.7	3.5	2.8
Senior secondary	1.7	1.5	1.0
Secondary plus training	13.8	14.6	13.8
Degree or higher	1.0	1.1	0.6
Total	100.0	100.0	100.0

Source: Calculated from table 6.11.

Botswana have assumed that the coefficients can be expected to be stable within sectors, over extended periods of time – i.e. up to 20 years. There is now sufficient information available in Botswana to test the efficacy of these assumptions.

Table 6.13 shows the ways in which the structure of educational qualifications required by jobs in the formal sector (excluding central government) changed over the years 1972-84. It is clear that there was a considerable upgrading of the required educational structure for jobs in the private and parastatal sectors. Whereas only about 11 per cent of jobs required JC or higher educational qualifications in 1972, more than one-quarter required such education in 1984. The upgrading was particularly concentrated at senior secondary levels – although both middle secondary and degree-level requirements increased at rates which were considerably faster than total employment. This can be seen from inspection of the elasticity estimates for the increased demand for educated workers with respect to total employment. They are shown in table 6.14.

Thus the demand for leavers at Form V increased more than twice as fast as total employment. Demand increases at Form 3 and degree levels exceeded employment growth by 84 per cent and 38 per cent, respectively, over the 12-year period. Thus, it is clear that to assume constant education and training coefficients over a long projection period would have been mistaken in the past, and would almost certainly remain so in the future.

These changes are, of course, a result of the interaction of both demand and supply effects. As educated people became available, so hiring standards rose; this is necessary to preserve the average ability level of recruits to given occupations. Similarly, as job tasks become more complicated, and/or require the application of different technologies, so the skill level of workers needs to rise. It is not possible to know the extent to which the particular supply or demand effects dominate. Nevertheless, the *general* shortage of skills, together with the apparent lack of growth in levels of labour productivity over the period, suggest that demand effects in Botswana are likely to have remained fairly strong causes of these phenomena.

It should be noted, moreover, that the proportion of the labour force employed in the formal sector increased from 10 per cent to 32 per cent over the

Table 6.13. Botswana, changing structure of educational qualifications required in the private, parastatal and local government sectors, 1972-84

	Less than Form 3	Form 3	Form 5/A level	Degree, post-graduate	Total
1972					
Batswana	23 779	1 481	439	29	25 728
Non-Batswana	1 225	458	489	201	2 373
Total	25 004	1 939	928	230	28 101
Per cent	89.0	6.9	3.3	0.8	100.0
1984					
Batswana	55 619	11 098	5 785	302	72 804
Non-Batswana	291	443	2 215	594	3 534
Total	55 910	11 541	8 000	896	76 338
Per cent	73.2	15.1	10.5	1.2	100.0
Ratio of totals 1984/1972	2.24	5.95	8.62	3.90	2.72
Average growth of totals 1972/84 (per cent)	6.9	16.0	19.7	12.0	8.7

Notes: 1972 data exclude all teachers; 1984 data exclude all teachers employed by the Central Government. Owing to problems arising from data collection, or interpretation, the 1984 survey understates degree-level requirements in the private and parastatal sectors. The estimates shown above are based upon information from the 1982 survey – grossed up to 1984 on the basis of the increase in total employment, by citizenship between 1982 and 1984. The estimates shown for jobs requiring Form 5/A-level in 1984 are reduced concomitantly with the increases made at degree level, in comparison with data in source.

Source: Ministry of Finance and Development Planning, 1973: *Manpower and Employment in Botswana*, table B8; Central Statistics Office: *Employment Survey 1982*, tables 9A-9C and *Employment Survey 1984*, tables 8A and 8C.

period. If one were to assume that the most able people were, throughout the period, those who found jobs, the *average* ability level of those in employment would have declined monotonically over time. Under those circumstances, the amount of education required to create a given level of skill can be expected to have *risen*, irrespective of changes in production structure and techniques, and irrespective of what happened to the supply of educated and trained persons over the intervening period.

Table 6.14. Botswana, education and training elasticities, actual, 1972/84, and as assumed in manpower plans

Level of education	Actual 1972-84	Assumed 1973	Assumed 1983-85
Less than Form 3	0.79	0.86	1.0
Form 3	1.84	1.30	1.0
Form 5/A levels	2.26	1.74	1.0
Degree	1.38	1.22	1.0

Note: Elasticities were calculated by dividing the average annual rate of growth of employment in jobs requiring each level of education shown, by the average annual rate of growth of formal employment.

4. Comparison of projections and outcomes

It would have been interesting to be able to compare all aspects of the projéc-tions of Botswana's successive manpower plans with the actual outcomes as revealed by subsequent history. In fact, this is only possible to a limited extent since the data on outcomes which are relevant to those plans published during the mid-1980s are not yet available. Moreover, the 1973 plan cannot be evaluated with respect to how well all its projections have fared, since the data do not exist in sufficient detail so to do. Never-theless, some comparisons are possible which allow generalizations about the chang-ing reliability of manpower forecasting in Botswana to be made.

Firstly, the medium-term forecasts of the 1973 plan proved to be rather satis-factory in a number of respects. Table 6.15 shows the sectoral composition of employ-ment for 1978 as projected in 1973 and as actually emerged. It can be seen that the forecast was closely accurate in aggregate terms (projected annual growth of 8.8 per cent, compared with 9 per cent actually achieved) and that in sectoral terms the esti-mates were also very respectable.

Secondly, the forecast of the growth of the government establishment to both 1978 and 1988 made in 1973 was also extremely accurate in total – being under-estimated by only 1 per cent and 3 per cent respectively (table 6.16). Even at the departmental level the estimates in the last column of the table must be viewed in most cases to be highly successful, given that a 15-year planning perspective was cov-ered by these projections.

Estimates of total employment to 1988 were not made in the 1973 report since these were thought to be too unreliable to justify publication. Equally, since employment data disaggregated by occupation and education are not available for 1988, further detailed assessment of reliability cannot at this stage be made. Never-theless the elasticity estimates used in the 1973 report, discussed above, imply that the overall projections of demand for skilled workers – defined in terms of education and economic sector – were not too wide of the mark, at least to 1978. The projec-tions to 1988 were, however, serious underestimates owing to the underestimation of the overall rate of economic growth which was to prove sustainable in Botswana over the long term.

As to the planning documents produced during the 1980s, underestimation of future demand for educated and trained people became much more serious. Even the medium-term projections of these documents were seriously flawed by their assuming that education and training coefficients would remain unchanged over time. The evidence presented above demonstrates that such assumptions are likely to be mistaken: irrespective of whether one believes demand or supply effects predom-inate in Botswana, the fact that so many (expensive) expatriates continue to be employed suggest that supply effects cannot yet be cited as the *general* cause of the upgrading of hiring standards. In the early 1970s, an assumption, for projection pur-poses, that demand for workers with senior secondary schooling and above would increase, in Botswana, at a multiple of up to twice the rate of growth of total employ-ment would have proved considerably more accurate than assuming that these vari-ables would increase at the same rate. It is safe to conclude, therefore, that the man-

Table 6.15. Botswana, projections of formal employment, 1973-78, and actual levels (000's)

Economic sector	Formal employment (actual)		Projected employment
	April 1972	August 1978	April 1978
Agriculture	5.1	5.2	6.7
Mining and quarrying	1.6	4.7	3.2
Manufacturing	2.6	5.7	5.7
Construction	6.5	9.2	8.7
Commerce and finance	6.3	11.0	10.7
Transport and communications	1.1	2.0	2.2
Local government	1.0	4.3	2.0
Education	3.4	6.1	4.5
Other services	3.2	4.7	5.0
Central government	93.3	16.6	18.1
Total	40.2	69.5	66.7

Source: for April 1972 and projections, Ministry of Finance and Development Planning, 1973: *Manpower and employment in Botswana*, table 1.5; for Aug. 1978, Central Statistical Office: *Employment Survey 1978*.

power plans published during the 1980s understated the likely future demands for educated and trained people by a substantial margin. Revised calculations based upon different assumptions indicate that the extent of underestimation of future demand could turn out to be as great as 50 per cent, even for their relatively short-period projections.

5. Conclusions

Taking the whole period 1965-90, it is clear that manpower plans in Botswana have fairly consistently underestimated the demand for professional, technical and other skilled workers, as revealed by subsequent employment outcomes. Over these years, the manpower shortage became more severe in important respects, and we can conclude that deficiencies in, and errors of, planning were partly to blame for this.

But at least as regards the estimation of employment trends, and of broad education and training categories, the story is by no means one of unmitigated disaster. The 1973 plan was more soundly based than its successors: its short-run projections appear to have been rather accurate, and its underestimation of demand in the long run mainly derived from the fact that the remarkably high rates of economic growth achieved over the 1980s were not anticipated by any of Botswana's economic planners (nor, indeed, by anyone else). If there are technical faults here, they lie more in the wider domain of economic forecasting than in that of manpower forecasting *per se*.

The performance of the set of manpower plans published during the 1980s was much worse. Here, the major error was to assume that the structure of educational and training qualifications held by the employed labour force would (and

Table 6.16. Botswana, established posts in central government: A comparison of actual and projected outcomes[1]

Ministry/Department	Actual posts 1972/73	Projected posts 1977/78	Actual posts 1977/78	Difference actual/projected 1977/78	Projected posts 1987/88			Actual posts 1987/88	Difference actual/projected 1987/88
					Low	High	Middle		
1 State President	234	298	422	1.42	441	586	514	654	1.27
2 Police	1 269	1 627	1 846	1.13	2 408	3 200	2 804	2 617	0.93
3 Finance and Planning	386	503	640	1.27	745	989	867	1 354	1.56
4 Health, Labour, Home Affairs	177	217	413	1.90	321	427	374	652	1.74
5 Medical Department	691	1 408	1 012	0.72	1 634	1 892	1 763	2 183	1.24
6 Prisons	193	213	355	1.67	315	419	367	875	2.38
7/8/9 Agriculture	1 014	1 868	1 218	0.65	2 635	3 191	2 913	2 005	0.69
10 Education[2]	89	148	215	1.45	219	291	255	702	2.75
11 Commerce and Industry	61	90	129	1.43	133	177	155	326	2.10
12 Wildlife, Survey, Water	382	636	628	0.99	941	1 251	1 096	981	0.90
13 Local Government and Lands	332	477	506	1.06	706	938	822	510[3]	0.62
14/15 Works and Communications	827	1 429	1 602	1.12	2 116	2 811	2 463	1 898[4]	0.77
16 Administrations of Justice	53	69	108	1.57	102	136	119	181	1.52
17 Adult	35	49	44	0.90	73	96	84	45	0.55
Total	5 743	9 032	9 138	1.01	12 789	16 404	14 597	14 984	1.03
Average annual growth (per cent)		9.48	9.73	1.03			4.92	5.07	1.03

[1] Owing to reorganization within the public service the composition of ministries and departments has often changed over the 15-year period. For purposes of the above comparison the groupings of 1972/73 have been held. This has involved reallocating some departments to ministries to which they did not later belong. [2] All teachers and school personnel are excluded from the comparison because they are included in the private/parastatal sector for purposes of the 1972 survey. [3] The very small recorded growth from 1977/78 -1987/8 is mainly because of the disbanding of the Department of Community Development in 1978. [4] Slow apparent growth caused by the Department of Telecommunications being re-established as a parastatal corporation in 1978.

Sources: Ministry of Finance and Development Planning, 1973: *Manpower and Employment in Botswana*, table F.2 and appendix F and data provided by the Department of Public Service Management, Gaborone.

should) remain unchanged over the planning period. Substitution of more realistic assumptions than these, informed by measurable trends in the labour market, would have reduced some of the worst sources of variation between what was projected, and what subsequently transpired.

This is not to argue, of course, that the detailed occupational forecasts of any of these plans has been closely accurate over periods longer than a few years. Those of the 1973 plan may have been, but data do not exist in a sufficiently disaggregated form to test this. Nevertheless it has been shown that the forecasting framework within which the more detailed projections were placed was effective in the case of the 1973 study. This is so both as regards the results of the employment projections and the assumptions adopted for the education/training density of future employment. The less satisfactory assumptions adopted by planners during the 1980s largely explain the deterioration in the efficacy of the forecasts published in recent years.

References

Colclough, C. 1976. "Some lessons from Botswana's experience with manpower planning", in *Botswana Notes and Records*, Vol. 8 (Gaborone).

Colclough, C. and S. McCarthy. 1980. *The political economy of Botswana: A study of growth and distribution* (Oxford, Oxford University Press).

Ministry of Finance and Development Planning (MFDP). 1983. *National Manpower Development Planning 1983*, 1984. *National Manpower Development Planning 1984*, 1985. *National Manpower Development Planning 1985*, 1990. National Development Plan (mimeo).

Republic of Botswana. 1966a. *The development of the Bechuanaland economy: Report of the Ministry of Overseas Development Economic Survey Mission*, November 1965 (Government Printer, Gaborone).

—. 1966b. *Transitional Plan for Social and Economic Development* (Government Printer, Gaborone).

—. 1968. *National Development Plan 1968-73* (Government Printer, Gaborone).

—. 1970. *National Development Plan 1970-75* (Government Printer, Gaborone).

—. 1973a. *Manpower and employment in Botswana* (Government Printer, Gaborone).

—. 1973b. *National Development Plan 1973-78* (Government Printer, Gaborone).

—. 1978. *Employment Survey 1978* (Central Statistics Office (CSO), Gaborone).

—. 1980. *National Migration Survey* (CSO, Gaborone).

—. 1981. *Population Census* (CSO, Gaborone).

—. 1983. *Employment Survey 1982* (CSO, Gaborone).

—. 1984. *Employment Survey 1984* (CSO, Gaborone).

—. 1984/5. *Labour Force Survey 1984-85* (CSO, Gaborone).

—. 1985. *National Development Plan 1985-91* (Government Printer, Gaborone).

—. 1987a. *Statistical Bulletin*, Vol. 12, No. 2 (CSO, Gaborone), June.

—. 1987b. *Statistical Bulletin*, Vol. 12, No. 1 (CSO, Gaborone), March.

—. 1987c. *Employment Survey 1986* (CSO Gaborone).

—. 1988. *Education Statistics 1988* (CSO, Gaborone).

—. 1989. *Labour Statistics 1988* (CSO, Gaborone).

—. 1990. *Report of the Presidential Commission on the Review of the Incomes Policy* (Government Printer, Gaborone).

Republic of Zambia. 1966. *Manpower Report* (Cabinet Office, Government Printer, Lusaka).

World Bank. 1990. *World Development Report 1990* (Washington, DC).

7.

Information needs for the transition to labour markets

Martin Godfrey*

1. Introduction

Transition from the allocation of labour by central planning to allocation by market forces is a traumatic process. In particular, it involves the emergence of open unemployment in place of low-productivity "unemployment on the job", and a resulting dramatic reduction in job and employment security. The management and minimization of this unfamiliar phenomenon depend on the availability of information. In addition, a widening of wage and income differentials, between workers of different skill and education levels, genders, ethnic groups and occupations, and between workers in different sectors, types of firm and regions, is likely to occur. The relative importance of small enterprises, self-employment, multiple employment and casual wage labour is likely to increase, as is movement of workers and jobseekers, between enterprises and from rural to urban and other rural areas. This paper briefly reviews the information that is needed for policy purposes in this situation, in comparison with what is usually available, drawing mainly on the experience of Hungary and China.

2. Unemployment

The first, obvious need is for information about the number and characteristics of the unemployed. As far as possible, these should be both not working and seeking work, in line with the usual definition of open unemployment. This may raise immediate problems, since it is very difficult to ensure that those who are registered as jobseekers are also not working; indeed, in Hungary [1] working for less than the minimum wage did not, at least until December 1991, disqualify a jobseeker from receiving benefit. Table 7.1, for Hungary, shows the type of data that are usually collected on unemployment, beneficiaries and vacancies. In developing countries registration systems are unlikely to be comprehensive, and such data may need to be supplemented from household labour force surveys.

* Institute of Development Studies, Sussex University, Brighton.
[1] For further discussion of the Hungarian case, see ILO, 1992.

Table 7.1. Hungary, trends in unemployment and vacancies, January 1990 – September 1991

Year/month	Registered unemployed (end of month)	Unemployment rate (per cent)	Receiving compensation (end of month)	Number of vacancies
1990				
Jan.	23 426	0.5	9 901	37 711
Feb.	30 055	0.6	13 603	38 335
Mar.	33 682	0.7	17 090	34 048
Apr.	33 353	0.7	20 037	35 191
May	38 155	0.8	22 295	37 938
June	43 506	0.9	25 875	37 859
July	45 055	0.9	29 334	36 222
Aug.	45 518	0.9	33 462	33 732
Sep.	56 115	1.2	37 579	26 969
Oct.	60 997	1.3	42 457	22 763
Nov.	69 982	1.5	49 668	17 150
Dec.	79 521	1.7	61 693	16 815
1991				
Jan.	100 526	2.1	76 866	12 949
Feb.	128 386	2.7	100 143	14 721
Mar.	144 840	3.0	116 029	13 583
Apr.	167 407	3.5	120 292	16 478
May	165 022	3.4	131 562	14 919
June	185 554	3.9	145 612	14 860
July	216 568	4.5	168 926	15 186
Aug.	251 084	5.2	192 402	14 124
Sep.	292 756	6.1	213 774	15 351

Source: National Labour Centre: *Labour market information*, 1991/7 and 1991/10.

Information from each unemployed jobseeker (including age, sex, location, education, training, skill level, previous jobs, type of job sought, benefits received) needs not only to be collected but also to be stored in such a way as to be quickly retrievable for multivariate analysis. Design of an active labour market policy depends on the availability of this kind of information. In practice, it is usually collected from jobseekers on registration but is subjected to no more than two-dimensional analysis, as in Table 7.2, also for Hungary.

Another source of information about unemployment is a household-based labour force survey. As part of the transition, several governments are introducing such surveys. In Hungary, for instance, a quarterly sample survey is beginning to collect individual records of household members, including information about economic activity, enabling a distinction to be made between the active unemployed (not working + seeking work) and the inactive unemployed (not working, not seeking but available for work). Such surveys are a useful check on the accuracy of unemployment registration records; in Hungary the pilot survey showed that many of those who claim benefit are not unemployed, and many of those who are unemployed are not claiming benefit.

Table 7.2. Hungary, characteristics of the registered unemployed, September 1991

Regional pattern

Region	Unemployment rate (per cent)	Region	Unemployment rate (per cent)
Budapest	1.8	Komáróm-E	5.5
Baranya	6.2	Nógrád	11.7
Bács-Kiskun	8.2	Pest	6.0
Békés	9.6	Somogy	6.4
Borsod-A-Z	10.1	Szabolcs-S-B	12.6
Csongrád	6.1	Tolna	8.1
Fejér	5.2	Vas	4.2
Györ-M-S	4.0	Veszprém	6.2
Hajdú-B	6.6	Zala	5.1
Heves	8.0	Overall	6.1
Jasz-N-S	9.1		

Education

Level	Per cent		Age group	
	All	School-leavers	Years	Per cent
<8 years	11	0.3	<17	1
8 years	35	5	17-20	15
Voc. school	31	45	21-25	14
Secondary	20	44	26-35	27
Higher	4	5	36-55	40
			>55	3
Total	100	100		100

Sex and skill level ('000)

Level	Male	Female	Total	Level	Male	Female	Total
Manual:				*Non-manual:*			
Skilled	42	10	52	Top managers	0.2	0.05	0.3
Semi-skilled	21	23	44	Middle mgrs	31	4	35
Unskilled	35	20	55	Lower mgrs	3	1	4
Total	99	53	152	Professional	5	8	13
				Clerical	3	10	13
				Total	13	20	34

Source: National Labour Centre: *Labour market information*, 1991/10.

Most governments are implementing active labour market programmes to ease the transition. Such programmes (often including training courses, assistance for prospective entrepreneurs, public works programmes, subsidised short-time working and job creation and early retirement schemes) need to be monitored and evaluated. This involves the collection of data not only about the number of participants in each type of programme, but also about costs and outcomes. In this respect, the use of a unique identification number for each registrant would be useful for tracing the subsequent labour market experience of the unemployed.

3. Employment

Information is needed about employment as well as unemployment. At the least, data on the number of wage employees, by sex, age, sector, occupation and skill level and ownership and size of establishment are needed. Table 7.3, for Hungary, shows the usual limits of the type of data that are easily retrievable, highly aggregated by sector and skill category and covering only establishments with 50 or more employees.

Most centrally planned economies collected huge amounts of data about establishments, through regular censuses. They now face the task of converting these unwieldy exercises, carried out infrequently and reported on, if at all, only after long delays, into more manageable sample surveys. In addition, coverage needs to be extended to smaller establishments and to the emerging private sector.

It would be useful also to have similar information about the number of self-employed, since this is likely to be the destination, particularly in the trade and services sectors, of many of those dismissed by state enterprises.

For these purposes, establishment surveys can be supplemented by the new household labour force surveys, although the data collected there on occupation, sector and type of establishment may be less reliable.

Short-time and surplus employees

Old practices of hoarding surplus workers die hard. State enterprises often put employees on short time in preference to laying them off immediately (this has been particularly so in Romania). In China some employees are officially designated as "surplus" prior to dismissal.

Information about short-time workers, again by sector, ownership and size of establishment, sex and skill level, is useful for employment policy, but is often not available. In Hungary, for instance, data are only available on those short-time workers for whom employers obtain wage subsidies from labour centres.

As for surplus employees, information about the official category is interesting, but it often understates by far the number that is surplus in relation to that needed to produce current levels of output.

Intended and actual dismissals

The number of officially designated surplus employees may correspond approximately to the number of intended dismissals. In Hungary, under the new Employment Act, an employer of at least 30 workers who intends to reduce his staff by at least 25 per cent or by not less than 50 workers within a period of six months has to notify his decision, three months prior to notice, to the labour centre and to the workers' organization at the workplace; and an employer who intends to lay off at least 10 workers must notify the workers concerned and the labour centre 30 days in advance. Table 7.4 shows the kind of statistics that can be retrieved from this process.

Table 7.3. Hungary, employment by sector, averages January to September 1991, and percentage change between 1990 and 1991

Economic sector	Manual		Non-manual		Total	
	'000	%	'000	%	'000	%
Industry, of which:	836.5	-12.1	236.4	-12.9	1 072.9	-12.3
Mining	54.7	-16.2	11.7	-18.2	66.4	-16.5
Electricity	28.4	-7.6	13.1	-3.7	41.5	-6.4
Metallurgy	41.5	-16.7	10.8	-18.2	52.3	-17.0
Engineering	242.5	-14.8	85.5	-16.7	328.0	-15.3
Building materials	41.3	-10.0	9.9	-11.7	51.2	-10.3
Chemical	70.4	-7.5	26.2	-4.5	96.6	-6.7
Light industry	198.6	-11.6	39.2	-13.0	237.8	-11.8
Food industry	145.4	-6.4	3.3	-7.5	182.1	-6.6
Construction	123.4	-20.6	44.8	-22.0	168.2	-21.0
Agriculture and forestry	372.4	-23.9	88.4	-19.0	460.8	-23.0
Transport, posts, telephone	211.3	-10.9	93.1	-6.5	304.4	-9.6
Trade	207.7	-15.6	118.5	-12.6	326.2	-15.1
Water	47.9	-14.4	13.0	-17.3	60.9	-15.1
Other	15.9	-30.3	7.8	-22.0	23.7	-27.8
Total, of which:	1 815.1	-15.9	602.0	-13.9	2 417.1	-15.4
Small/medium[1] establishments	362.7	-0.4	117.2	+2.4	479.9	+0.3
Large establishments[2]	1 452.4	-19.1	484.8	-17.1	1 937.2	-18.6

[1] 50-300 employees. [2] More than 300 employees.

Source: Kozponti Statiztikai Hivatal: *Az anyagi agak munkaugyi jellemzoi*, 1991, I-III negyedev.

Table 7.4. Hungary, expected dismissals from September 1991 to February 1992, as reported by employers ('000)

1991	
September	13.7
October	17.1
November	9.8
December	10.6
1992	
January	1.7
February	0.03
Unknown timing	25.5
Total	78.3

Source: as for table 7.1.

Table 7.5. Hungary, average gross wages by sector, January-September 1991 (Ft '000 per month) and percentage change between 1990 and 1991

Economic sector	Manual		Non-manual		Total	
	Ft '000	%	Ft '000	%	Ft '000	%
Industry, of which:	14.2	29.7	22.6	35.7	16.1	31.4
Mining	23.2	38.9	36.6	51.6	25.5	41.7
Electricity	16.4	35.2	24.8	38.1	19.1	36.8
Metallurgy	17.0	26.1	25.4	32.6	18.7	27.7
Engineering	13.3	28.8	20.6	35.4	15.2	30.8
Building materials	13.8	27.6	21.9	34.7	15.3	29.1
Chemical	17.3	36.3	26.9	37.6	20.0	37.2
Light industry	11.0	26.0	19.5	30.9	12.4	26.8
Food industry	14.0	27.7	21.8	30.9	15.6	28.4
Construction	13.4	20.4	22.9	27.4	16.0	22.6
Agriculture and forestry	10.3	19.4	17.3	22.6	11.7	20.8
Transport, posts, telephone	14.8	36.4	19.9	40.5	16.4	38.3
Trade	11.3	31.1	22.4	34.3	15.5	33.4
Water	13.7	29.2	21.5	32.3	15.4	29.7
Other	10.8	23.6	21.8	29.8	14.6	29.0
Average, of which:	13.1	28.7	21.3	33.4	15.2	30.5
Small/medium establishments[1]	11.3	22.8	20.6	29.1	13.6	25.3
Large establishments[2]	13.5	30.5	21.5	34.4	15.5	32.1

[1] 50-300 employees   [2] More than 300 employees.

Source: Kozponti Statiztikai Hivatal: *Az anyagi agak munkaugyi jellemzoi*, 1991, I-III negyedev.

The absence of reliable data on actual dismissals is a big gap in labour market information, but, according to county labour centres, 90 to 95 per cent of planned dismissals are carried out. No information is available, either, about dismissals of groups of less than ten workers, thought to be a significant proportion of the total, nor about the sex, age and occupation of those to be dismissed, nor the sector in which the establishment is operating. Nevertheless, though imperfect, the dismissal figures represent a useful "early warning" system.

Wages and earnings

Data on wages and earnings are needed as indicators of the extent to which a labour market is emerging. Differentials, between workers of different skill and education levels, genders, ethnic groups and occupations, and between workers in different sectors, types of firm and regions, are usually low in previously centrally planned economies, even when allowances and fringe benefits are taken into account. They can be expected to increase as a market develops, and this process (usefully increasing incentives to relevant skill acquisition, productivity increase and labour mobility but with obvious negative aspects and possibly tending to overshoot) needs to be monitored. Trends in unskilled wages, also, are a useful guide to the state of the lower end of the labour market.

Streamlined establishment surveys will presumably still contain questions about wages, but these are usually at a highly aggregated level and relevant mainly to the measurement of labour costs. Much more useful, particularly for analysis of differentials, are data based on individual records of workers. Household labour force surveys sometimes ask about wages, but such data (often collected from proxy informants) are less reliable than information collected in the workplace. One interesting possibility is to select a sample of individuals from establishments' payrolls. In Hungary, where such a survey is at the pilot stage, the compact questionnaire contains a line for each individual, selected on the basis of birth-date. The resulting information on sex, occupation, education, hours worked, wage, allowances, fringe benefits, combined with information on the establishment, will be extremely useful for monitoring labour markets. Meanwhile all that can be gleaned from current wage statistics is the highly aggregated trends shown in table 7.5.

4. Monitoring labour market reform through special surveys

It may be useful to combine some of the features of the usual establishment survey with the collection of individual records on workers, in order to monitor the process of labour market reform. A pilot survey for this purpose was carried out in China in 1987.[2] A sample[3] of 109 state, collective and individual enterprises in the construction, transportation, commerce, agriculture and manufacturing sectors was surveyed in the city of Shashi in Hubei province. Individual records were collected on nearly 36,000 workers in the enterprises.

The questionnaire used in the survey was in two parts. Part A asked for details about the establishment, including form of ownership, sector of main activity, whether it had a labour service company, output, profits, taxation, employees by nature of contract, age and sex, cash payments to employees, numbers hired and numbers left, number of vacancies, number of surplus employees, employees and surplus employees by skill category, and details about training and vacancies. At the same time, Part B asked for an individual record of each employee in the establishment, covering sex, age, length of time with establishment, initial grade, current grade, channel of recruitment to first appointment, occupation, employment status, education, training, basic wage and salary, bonuses and other cash payments, and welfare benefits received from the enterprise.

This combination of information about the establishment and individual records enabled a large number of questions to be addressed, including the following (with answers, highly summarized, in brackets):

---

[2] See ILO, 1988, for further details of this survey.
[3] Representing a 26 per cent sample of state and a 30 per cent sample of collective enterprises.

- What progress have enterprises of different kinds made in labour market reform? (Not much in any kind of enterprise, to judge from a range of indicators, including incidence of different types of contracts, channels of recruitment, dismissals, resignations, surplus workers and vacancy rates.)

- Does the type of manager in charge of a state or collective enterprise make any difference to its progress with labour market reform? (No, but more educated managers achieve consistently higher profit per employee.)

- Which occupational groups have the highest rate of surplus employees and which the lowest? (This turned out to be a relatively meaningless question, because "surplus employee" was taken to mean the official category rather than those surplus in relation to the minimum number required to produce the current level of output.)

- In which occupational categories are there critical shortages? (Production and transport workers, mainly in the manufacturing sector.)

- In which occupational categories is there the highest rate of vacancies and with what educational and work experience requirements? (In general, engineering technologists and technicians, with evidence of qualifications escalation and of internal labour markets.)

- To what extent have current employees (particularly those in higher grades and positions) risen through the ranks of the enterprise? (In general, to a large extent, even in the case of deputy managers, but to a lesser extent in the case of managers.)

- How do training facilities and procedures vary between state and collective enterprises of different sizes? (Only the larger enterprises, and particularly state enterprises, employ full-time trainers and have training schools.)

- How does type of contract vary between different occupational groups? (Differentially, with almost all of professional and managerial workers still on lifetime contracts, and with short/temporary contracts concentrated among service and production workers and, particularly, construction workers.)

- How does type of contract vary between different age groups? (The young are overrepresented among those on contract and temporary terms.)

- How do wages vary between people of different sexes, educational backgrounds and age groups? (Significantly between men and women of the same age and educational background, less so between other categories, with seniority rather than education an important determinant of differentials.)

- How do wages vary between people in different occupations and of different ages? (Not much, at least in comparison with other countries.)

- What difference does training of different types make to the wages of lower secondary school graduates? (Only pre-employment training seems to make any difference, maybe for institutional reasons.)

- How does eligibility for employee welfare benefits vary between people of different sexes and ages, and by form of enterprise ownership? (With a consistent bias against females, younger workers, and those outside state enterprises.)

- How does eligibility for welfare benefits vary between people in different occupations? (Considerably, with certain élite occupations enjoying favoured coverage.)
- What are the characteristics of the individual sector? (Cash incomes are much higher and differentials wider than in state and collective enterprises, and the average enterprise is tiny.)

Several methodological lessons were learned from the pilot survey. The sample of state and collective enterprises would not need to be so large, and, within each enterprise sampled, individual records should be collected from a sample of employees rather than from all employees. On the other hand the sample of individual enterprises needs to be much larger. Some of the questions in the questionnaire need to be rethought. Most important for the purposes of monitoring labour market reform, some way of covering those who are not covered by an establishment survey, i.e. the unemployed (called "job waiters" in China) and those engaged casually or part-time in unregistered activities, has to be found. In the absence of a comprehensive system of unemployment benefit, the most scientific way of reaching these people may be through the kind of household labour force survey discussed above. If this were thought to be too expensive, a second-best approach would have to be devised.

5. Conclusions

In general, the pressure on resources that is involved in the transition to labour markets, particularly if it coincides with deep recession as it does in Eastern Europe, means that there will be little scope for ambitious new statistical initiatives. The emphasis, rather, should be on rationalization and improvement. Abolition of many of the old, massive, data-gathering censuses, oriented towards long-term planning and bureaucratic control, can release resources for quick and inexpensive sample surveys, oriented towards helping to understand how markets are working. Without such an understanding, the transition to labour markets will take more time and involve more pain than is necessary.

References

ILO. 1992. *Economic transformation and employment in Hungary* (Geneva, ILO).
ILO-ARTEP. 1988. *Labour market reforms in China*, Report on Pilot Manpower Survey in Shashi City, Hubei Province, Asian HRD Planning Network (RAS/86/071) (New Delhi, ILO/ARTEP).

8

Proceedings of the workshop

Session 1. Manpower planning and analysis: An issues paper

In presenting the ILO paper *Peter Richards* (ILO) reviewed the development of manpower planning and related tools of analysis, and the part they have played in influencing government action on issues of education, training and labour allocation. He traced the changing concepts of manpower planning and agreed that however it may have worked in the past, whether through anticipating or forecasting demand for skills irrespective of market signals or through determining rates of return to educational levels, current thinking was on very different lines. Corresponding to the increased emphasis put on market-oriented systems of resource allocation, current slogans in manpower analysis pinpointed such concepts as transparency in labour markets and reward systems, and flexibility of acquired education and training rather than numerical accuracy in forecasting. The new approach also strongly played down the role of the government, and suggested that publicly subsidizing skill acquisition was not necessary. In this "decentralized paradigm" the role of the government was much more limited and was concentrated on the following five areas: (a) to correct for any distorting effects of its own policies on the conditions under which individual, including enterprise, decisions on skill acquisition and labour allocation are taken; (b) to increase the horizontal equity of access to finance; (c) to guide the skill acquisition process; (d) to increase the flexibility of its own "in-house" skill acquisition and labour allocation process; and (e) to take decisions on the relation of social to private benefits in this process and act upon them through expenditure and revenue decisions. *Peter Richards* concluded by saying that manpower planning units in government should be less involved with planning vocational training and more involved with issues of problem identification and solving and that the ILO should help them in such a direction.

There was no general discussion on the issues paper.

Session 2. Macroeconomic and manpower planning issues

In introducing his paper entitled "Manpower planning and economic development", *Robert Lucas* (Boston University) maintained that manpower planning had been mainly seen as an alternative to relying on market forces. He, however, raised the question that if markets, in theory at least, were meant to clear the balance between the demand and supply for skills then why should manpower planning be necessary. He thought that the main reasons stemmed either from efficiency considerations or from a wish to provide equality of opportunities or outcomes. On grounds of efficiency the most common sphere in which positive externalities were discussed was with respect to basic education as it was argued that an educated population might take decisions which would benefit them in a number of dimensions which might not be reflected in any pricing mechanism (e.g. educated women leading to lower fertility rates). The lack of information could also lead to inefficient private decisions.

On the interconnections between skills, trade and development strategy, both in the context of static comparative advantage and in a dynamic, changing world, *Robert Lucas* was of the view that, on the whole, intervention in the form of manpower planning was not necessary to build up comparative advantage through the development of skilled manpower. However, as illustrated by the newly industrialized countries of East Asia, a case could be made for deliberately investing in training to establish a comparative advantage in a specific industry. This could either be justified on the grounds of externalities and on trying to achieve a high equilibrium growth trajectory, or on the more traditional infant industry grounds of capital market failures or learning externalities and hence insufficient investment in training. But he warned that this could also be a risky strategy with potentially high costs as many countries which had promoted infant industries in the past had discovered. In a world of flux it was very difficult for a country to forecast with any accuracy the future set of industries in which it was likely to be more competitive. This state of flux had profound implications for the appropriate design of a manpower strategy.

Robert Lucas stated that if on grounds of equity, efficiency and design of strategy there were legitimate reasons for wanting to intervene in the private training market, then the important question related to the form that these interventions might take. In this regard a broad distinction needed to be made between the role of the State in offering financial incentives and support in education and training and in its role as a provider of training, though of course the two often overlapped.

As regards the financing of education on the grounds of promoting greater equality within and across generations, *Robert Lucas* argued that a higher rate of subsidy seemed warranted for basic than for tertiary level education. As to the grounds on which public authorities should take these decisions, *Robert Lucas* was of the view that both the manpower planning approach as well as rate-of-return analysis were seriously flawed. While both offered some interesting insights, the rigid application of either would be a mistake. In the end a careful review of the current performance of the educational system needed to be conducted with a view to discerning spheres for improvement in the light of the overall development strategy. As regards state involvement in training, he felt that it was not obvious that the public sector had any innate advantage in organizing training and in fact private sector training facilities were not uncommon. Where, however, training was organized by the public sector it was crucial to involve employers in decisions with respect to the fields of training and even in the design of that training.

Discussion

The discussion on Robert Lucas's paper centred on four major themes, namely: (1) whether the role of government in manpower planning varied according to the stage of a country's development; (2) the relationship between human resources development and economic performance; (3) the need to take into account international movements of labour in human resource planning; and (4) the role of a manpower planning unit in human resources development (HRD) planning.

Christopher Colclough (Institute of Development Studies, Sussex University) pointed out that the key area of debate was the type and form of intervention that was required by the government in developing the country's human resources. If it was accepted that the whole world was not the same and that developing countries suffered far more from market imperfections and failures then there could be a case for government intervention in such countries. Also, substitution possibilities were far lower in developing countries and this situation was worsened by the lack of available information. Similarly, while in industrialized economies quantitative forecasting issues might not be important, this again was not true for all the developing countries. In the United Kingdom, for instance, it was unnecessary to project the demand for engineers – the same was not true for example for Burkina Faso. *Christopher Colclough* argued that in such circumstances manpower planning might be important and needed to be based on a combination of manpower projections and rate-of-return analysis.

A number of participants disagreed with Mr. Colclough that developed countries were all that different from the developing countries when it came to manpower planning. *Robert Lucas* enquired whether small developing countries were different from the larger ones and was dismissive of size being a major issue in this debate. He did not believe that lack of substitution possibilities could be traced to market failures. *Martin Godfrey* (Institute of Development Studies, Sussex University) also maintained that substitutability was in many cases far greater than was envisaged by Colclough. He gave the example of Indonesia where deregulation of the financial sector had led to shortages of accountants but this demand had been met by retraining other professionals. *Bo Hermen* (Pakistan/Netherlands Project on Human Resources) pointed out that the pace of change was not as fast as was made out in Robert Lucas's paper and that the demand for skills was more stable and in this sense more predictable. *Robert Lucas* responded to this that Malaysia had given him a very different perspective.

The relationship between human resources development and economic growth, especially in the context of the NICs, also generated considerable discussion.

Martin Godfrey pointed out that this link has not been proven and cited Behrman's recent work.[1] The Philippines and Sri Lanka were examples of this high HRD and low growth mainly because of a wrong policy environment. Thailand with a relatively lower HRD base had witnessed very high growth, especially in recent years. *Christopher Colclough* supported the viewpoint that cause and effect were difficult to sort out in examining the success of the East Asian economies. Different countries responded very differently to sharp liberalization and the opening up of the economy. For example this had led to a virtual paralysis and a breakdown of the economy in Zimbabwe with very little switching of resources. *Robert Lucas* agreed that there was an enormous amount not known but he would not be dismissive of the role of HRD in economic development. He asked whether there was some relationship between HRD and the ability of NICs to pick out "winners" in terms of choice of industries which had performed so well in the export markets. A number of countries including Thailand were trying to emulate the East Asian experience.

Samir Radwan (ILO) raised the issue of the increasing globalization of the labour market and the transfer of professionals and skilled labour across international boundaries. *Robert Lucas* felt that since the numbers involved were a very small proportion of the annual increase in total world labour force the impact was not that significant. Also data on international labour flows was very sketchy. *Swapna Mukopadhya* (Institute of Economic Growth, New Delhi) pointed out that in certain categories of professionals the numbers leaving a country could be a significant proportion of the total, as for example in India where almost 50 per cent of Indian graduates from the prestigious Indian Institute of Technology (IIT) found employment abroad, mainly in the United States. *John Lawrence* (UNDP, New York) pointed out that international migration raised a number of interesting issues for manpower planning as well as that of who pays for the training of migrant workers and who benefits from it. Also the skill content of those migrating could cause shortages in the labour-sending countries, as for example happened in the large-scale migration to the Gulf countries from South Asia and South-East Asia.

George Psacharopoulos (World Bank) raised the issue of the role of a manpower planning unit in overall manpower planning decisions, for example, on the question of subsidizing primary education. *Robert Lucas* pointed out that his paper had a wider focus. The real challenge was how to broaden the present role of such units especially since existing officials were mostly old-fashioned manpower planners and were not the best placed to carry out the kind of analytical work that was required and was being suggested. The problem was that educational planners were unaware of labour market issues and at best paid it lip service. On the other hand labour market economists were either not aware or gave low priority to educational planning issues. *Swapna Mukopadhya* pointed out that the institutional set-up for manpower planning was important and that a manpower planning unit could be a useful source of information.

Samir Radwan pointed out that the underlying model for manpower planning had always been very simplistic. There was a need for developing a framework

---

[1] Behrman, Jere R. 1990. *Human resource-led development? Review of issues and evidence* (ILO/ARTEP, New Delhi).

that would encompass the important issues and in the process make manpower planning more meaningful and realistic. A problem faced in developing countries was that market signals were not always forthcoming – especially in the non-formal sector. Moreover, markets were interlinked and this made matters more complicated. *George Psacharopoulos*, however, contended that even the informal markets provided necessary signals and *Robert Lucas* also pointed out that in the informal sector markets do exist. *Samuel Cohen* (Dynamics Growth Institute, Rotterdam) pointed out that micro approaches give more insights than macro and there was a need for micro emphasis in policymaking.

Session 3. Lessons from regional and country experience

In the six papers presented, the experiences of the Asian and African regions and of Botswana, Pakistan, China and the Netherlands were assessed for possible lessons in developing new approaches to manpower planning and analysis.

The Botswana paper presented by *Christopher Colclough* concluded that planners had done relatively well in predicting the overall rate of economic growth and of employment at the macro level. However, detailed forecasts by occupation and educational level had proved less accurate, largely because of the inadequacy of data on which to base such forecasts, and for that reason should not be attempted.

As shown in the paper presented on the African region by *Eleazar Iwuji* (ILO), many governments persisted in forecasting manpower using the discredited manpower requirements approach, due to its attraction in helping achieve the localization of jobs. It was argued that a preferable approach would be to use manpower analysis and a reliable labour market information system was needed to carry out such analysis. In general, as noted by one participant, there had been a recent resurgence of interest in manpower planning in many African countries (Nigeria, Zambia, Zimbabwe), after having fallen from favour some 30 years ago. However, it was maintained that governments still mainly take *ad hoc* measures in response to concerns about unemployment.

In the presentation of his case study on Pakistan, *Bo Hermen* argued that the objective of manpower planning should be to shore up policies via the monitoring of the labour market and to enable policymakers to advise the decision-makers of the country. He felt in this exercise that there was a role for the Ministry of Labour – whose duties in Pakistan included manpower planning, but that the problem was how to equip the Ministry to carry out such responsibilities.

The paper on China by *Martin Godfrey* raised questions for a country in transition to a market economy. Was labour market flexibility just for the purpose of raising productivity or was it to reduce the influence of labour by creating a reserve army of the unemployed? How could the first objective be achieved without creating unemployment? With wage and salary differentials so narrow, how could the labour market alone be expected to allocate labour? The main thrust of the paper on the Netherlands' experience by *Samuel Cohen* in manpower planing was that the minimum wage was so close to the level of unemployment benefits that it left the low-skilled with little incentive to work.

Discussion

In the general discussion of the country papers, one participant maintained that there was room for government intervention in the labour market, since there was agreement on where and why the market has failed. Analysis of problems experienced in the labour market could lead to corrective actions. The need was to identify the activities involved in human resources planning and decide who should carry them out and for whom and when, and where the government should intervene. What were the problems? Who were the end-users of the analysis? What were the trade-offs between labour relations and employment and between growth and employment? Then what was to be done about the problems? Since it was important to have a long-term view of changes in the economic structure in order to allocate for the future, forecasting was necessary. But forecasting by whom and for whom?

Another participant agreed that more focus was needed on analysis than on methodology. As regards methodology, it was argued by another participant that more concern was needed with variability rather than defending particular approaches. A system should be developed and sited to spot the changes in the labour market that were occurring at a rapid pace.

In general, it was concluded that most countries were still wrestling with the intractable problem of filling in gaps in their institutional capacities and that their efforts in manpower analysis so far had tended to be one-off affairs.

Session 4. New approaches of manpower planning and analysis

George Psacharopoulos (World Bank) presenting his paper entitled "From manpower planning to labour market analysis" made a strong plea for a shift from what he termed traditional, old-fashioned, blind alley activities in the area of manpower planning, towards a set of more promising venues in labour market analysis. He listed a number of do's and don'ts in labour market analysis.

In his presentation *George Psacharopoulos* especially emphasized the need to analyse inefficiencies and distortions existing in the present system and in this regard noted that the collection of wage data would assist in pointing out how distorted was the existing incentive system. There was need to establish the free price of labour. He pointed out for example that attempts through enterprise surveys in China to identify skill and training needs could not be very helpful as there were no incentives in the system to encourage labour mobility. The real problem was that manpower planners did not understand "prices" and "costs" and therefore rarely analysed whether investments in skill development would raise productivity. There was need to assess the existing inefficiencies in labour use and analyse the extent to which they were caused by labour market distortions and government regulations.

George Psachrapoulos pointed out the need and advantages of imparting sound general training as against specialist school-based training, which, amongst its other advantages, would also facilitate the process of structural adjustment. He felt it was also essential to recover the costs of training, and to find out the extent to which individuals were prepared to pay for their own training. Also, there was need to shift the balance and concentrate on the present rather than to be obsessed with planning for the long-term future.

Discussion

Participants generally felt that the paper was deliberately provocative to generate fresh thinking on the subject. *Robert Lucas* said that it was an oversimplification to designate everything about manpower planning as *bad* and everything about labour market analysis as *good*. The key issue was deciding upon the appropriate form of labour market analysis and identifying its hard techniques which could be handled by manpower planning units. As regards some of the specific do's and don'ts in labour market analysis, a lot could still be done through enterprise surveys which Psacharopoulos had discouraged. Similarly, tracer studies, which he supported, could also be misleading and dangerous and produce biased results especially if they did not cover the unemployed. The point to grasp was that one set of data was normally not adequate to give the answers. As to relying on private institutions alone for training there was a problem of establishing the credibility of such institutions. Indeed one had to seriously pursue the issue of how well the private sector could organize training on its own. There were a large number of "fly-by-night" institutions. In any case, training through the private sector would still need government guidance and a system of national certification. Also as regards concentrating mainly on the short term it had to be kept in mind that labour market analysis was not necessarily short-term in nature. Some contracts were implicitly long term and hard to change e.g. in Japanese firms.

Christopher Colclough pointed out that the paper itself raised a number of "old" issues such as cost recovery of training and user fees related issues. User fees systems need to be combined with loans for those in need. He was more in favour of payroll taxes to collect educational dividends. One should not overlook the costs of not intervening at all.

In introducing his paper entitled "Planning for vocational education, training and employment: A minimalist approach", *Martin Godfrey* indicated that he wanted to emphasize the practical concerns in defining the scope and content of planning for employment and training. In keeping with a minimum use of planning resources and utilizing them efficiently, he argued for leaving all *short-term* (up to three years) planning for skill-generation to those who implement training programmes, which should be allowed to function on a self-regulating basis. Planners would merely restrict themselves to a coordinating role and would focus attention on monitoring and evaluating the training system based on techniques of labour market analysis.

For the *long term* (three years and over), *Martin Godfrey* argued that planning was necessary, and should be based on the rate-of-return analysis adjusted for expected structural changes in the economy. He maintained that the focus of such an exercise should not be on occupations, but on the type of skills, as statistics on occupations were very poor. If one carried out tracer studies to follow the fate of school-leavers in the labour market and did some cost analysis of the courses followed, one could calculate a rate of return for each course.

As regards structural change, as detailed a picture as possible should be built up, especially on the growing and shrinking sectors of the economy. There would also be implications for human resource development for countries trying to reshape their comparative advantage. For the public sector, utilizing a high percentage of high-level manpower, a detailed projection of labour demand should be prepared based on expected government revenue. For the private sector, the focus of the exercise should be on graduate-intensive industries.

Martin Godfrey urged that his proposed approach be followed as a continuing process, not as a one-off exercise. In summary, the minimalist scenario called for the manpower planners to collect and generate information and base their analysis on such information.

Discussion on the paper centred around two issues (a) the role of manpower planning, particularly as it related to skill generation and (b) the roles of the public vs. the public sector in training.

It was generally agreed that there *was* a need for a new approach in manpower planning, its objective would be to support the formulation of manpower policies. For instance, planning for the purpose of policy formulation for the development of human resources via education and training *was* needed, including on such issues as the choice of alternative training systems. In this case, manpower planning would be more closely linked with planning for the provision of training, which had not been the case so far. While planning for short-term skill generation programmes might not be necessary, as argued by Godfrey's minimalist approach, some planning *was* needed to prepare the skills required to develop such short-term training programmes.

The participants were split on the question of public vs. private training. While *George Psacharopoulos*, supported to some extent by *Martin Godfrey*, felt that short- and long-term training alike should be turned over to the private sector, with public money to finance general education only, and leaving the public to utilize or reject private training schools, other participants were sceptical. One maintained that private employers were basically uninterested in training and preferred to poach workers from other employers to meet their skill needs. Under such circumstances, how could training become self-regulating? Indeed, the capability of the private sector in training might have been overestimated, considering that the industry base in developing countries is usually too small to provide training within industry. Given the lack of experience of the private sector establishments in training programmes, how would on-the-job training alone be expected to meet skill needs? It was unrealistic to expect the private sector to be able to generate the supply of skilled labour that labour demand called for. Giving the private training institutions a greater role in providing training was not felt to be the answer either, since such institutions were often not responsible and did not always provide useful qualifications for their students.

In conclusion, it was felt that perhaps the optimum arrangement was for a partnership between the government and the private sector. Under this scenario, the government's role would be to actively support skill formation in the private sector (including for informal sector enterprises) while maintaining some skill training programmes of its own.

Session 5. Labour market information

In presenting her paper entitled "Information dissemination systems in the functioning of labour markets in developing countries: A case study of India", *Swapna Mukhopadhya* identified two basic problems in India for which labour market information was required: chronic manpower shortages and the malfunctioning of labour markets. The persistence in India of unfilled vacancies alongside the existence of educated unemployed were manifestations of these problems. Inadequate employment opportunities for women was another prob- lem. As regards data and information needs, there was the problem of how to define unemployment and in the case of the informal sector, the absence of the data required.

Rashid Amjad (ILO), observed that the dearth of labour market informa- tion and problems in its collection were not limited to India. Indeed, India had made an early start in the measurement of unemployment, but not many countries had fol- lowed its lead. Curiously, the level of unemployment in India as revealed by official surveys did not show much fluctuation regardless of economic conditions in the coun- try. As regards the collection of labour market information, it was noted that constant changes introduced by countries in the design of survey questionnaires made the comparability of results from surveys difficult over time.

In the discussion, *George Psacharopoulos* cited India as a classic example of the failure of "grandiose planning" and questioned why the country kept producing such plans. He also argued that instead of just collecting the numbers of the unem- ployed, data on income and wage levels were needed in order to identify persons below the poverty level, a more meaningful consideration than the numbers of unem- ployed. Another participant noted that the unemployed typically did not refer to the employment service for work and urged better labour market monitoring, including on the effects of structural adjustment programmes, which resulted in retrenchments in the public sector.

Section 6. Panel discussion

The concluding session of the workshop was a panel discussion of what the Chairperson, *Eddy Lee* (ILO), described as the "unresolved issues" which had emerged from the previous sessions. The other panel members were *Robert Lucas, Martin Godfrey, Christopher Colclough* and *George Psacharopoulos*. However, other participants joined in the debate.

Eddy Lee started the discussion by posing the following questions:

(i) What amount of planning for manpower development was desirable? Also was it only a question of less planning or a different type of planning?

(ii) Could manpower planning be completely replaced by labour market analysis and if so would such analysis be sufficient to deal with all the issues and tasks tra- ditionally performed by manpower planners? Did we need to analyse other interlinkages in the economy beyond those captured by the labour market?

(iii) What precisely was the role of intervention in the labour market? Was it simply confined to the removal of labour market distortions? Also, how did we take into account the fact that many distortions will take time to eliminate and that it may also not be possible to dismantle all distortions? What are the costs of non-intervention in the labour market? Indeed some interventions may be beneficial and ethically desirable on social and equity grounds.

The panel discussion as well as the views of the participants on these questions and other issues could be broadly divided into three broad groups. The first was the role, if any, of traditional manpower projections in this new approach to manpower planning and analysis. The second related to the role of labour market analysis and in what ways and in concrete terms it could replace the traditional approach. The third set of issues related to the institutional machinery for manpower planning and the kind of activities and analysis that a Manpower Planning Unit (in the Planning or Labour Ministry) could undertake to lead to the better utilization of human sources and to minimize skill mismatch in the economy.

On the first question related to the traditional manpower projections approach there was almost complete agreement that the more quickly it was disposed of as a tool for manpower analysis the better it would be. *George Psacharopoulos* made a strong plea for the ILO to issue a statement especially directed at its field units that manpower planning in terms of projecting numbers was worthless and if they were still undertaking this activity (even in response to specific government requests) to stop doing so. He gave the example of the World Bank which had recently made a major shift in its educational planning policy and was now advocating that there should be no vocationalization of academic courses. The only qualifications to this almost unanimous rejection of projecting numbers were made by *Christopher Colclough* and *Samuel Cohen*. *Christopher Colclough* stated that some quantitative questions would still need to be answered especially where numbers involved (for whom education or training facilities were to be provided) were particularly small and when key decisions on educational financing had to be undertaken. *Samuel Cohen* stated that the rejection of the manpower project approach did not imply that no numbers on the growth of the labour force would be generated. Clearly demographic projections and other implications of the growth of the population on age structure would need to be analysed. However, Cohen's point was not contested mainly since the discussion centred on projections of manpower needs by levels of occupation, education or skills.

On the question of what technique or methodology should replace the traditional manpower projections approach, there was a broad consensus that the major emphasis should be on labour market analysis. However, there were significant differences amongst the panellists on what exactly needed to be done under this approach and the extent to which one should leave the development and allocation of human resources simply to labour market signals.

George Psacharopoulos's view, which represented one extreme, was that manpower planning should concentrate on the way prices (i.e. wages) were behaving and not as he put it on "the counting of heads". When shortages of particular skills appeared, the best way of meeting them was to provide the right incentives in terms of wages and incomes. This was especially true of the public sector where in most cases shortages reflected very low wages and incomes offered rather than a real dearth of that particular skill or occupation in the economy.

Others, however, felt that there was need to go beyond analysis of the labour market alone to tackle manpower issues. *Robert Lucas* shared this view but emphasized that labour market analysis still provided a sufficient agenda to serve as an alternative to traditional manpower planning. *Christopher Colclough* felt that the approach to be adopted should also take into account the historical experience of countries as well as their role in the international economy. There was a need to carry out work on the historical evolution of the labour market and the need to analyse the employment problem in the context of the growth and structure of the productive sectors in relation to the structure of human resources. Especially important in this context was the need to analyse trends in wages and real incomes. Also in the 1990s focus must increasingly shift to an analysis of the labour market impact of structural adjustment and a review of successful and unsuccessful experiences. There was also a need to analyse the cost of distortions, especially those which were not the result of policy interventions.

George Psacharopoulos did not agree with the view that the methodology for manpower planning should differ for different countries; the basic methodological principles should apply to all countries as basically there is "only one theory" though the issues to be considered may be different. He did, however, endorse the view that there was a lot to learn from the historical evolution of labour markets.

Martin Godfrey raised the pertinent issue as to why monitoring and labour market analysis should be undertaken. The main reasons which he emphasized were to provide information for school-leavers and first-time jobseekers and to tackle the important questions related to underutilization of labour. He was of the opinion that the key information to monitor the state of the labour market was wage data as employment conceptually was very difficult to measure. *George Psacharopoulos* agreed and said this was the reason why the World Bank had stopped reporting unemployment data in its country reports. *Martin Godfrey* also emphasized the need to collect data on productivity. Overall, he was of the view that there was strong need to radically reorient the present data collected on labour markets. Overambition and carrying out too many surveys at the same time lead both to delays and difficulty in data processing. The costs and benefits of collecting information needed to be carefully evaluated.

The consensus seemed to move towards identifying critical issues especially those related to skill mismatch and the underutilization of labour resources. In this context *Robert Lucas* also mentioned the need to emphasize policy aspects in the design and implementation of projects and studies related to human resources development. He pointed out that in many cases policymakers were disappointed with detailed investigative studies on different aspects of the labour market because they did not come up with concrete policy conclusions. He gave the example of the recently completed UNDP/ILO project in Malaysia on HRD planning which had run into this problem.

An important issue raised during the discussion was the extent to which labour market analysis, and especially labour market indicators such as wages, would capture the role and needs of the informal sector. While some discussants (especially *Robert Lucas*) thought that this sector was best left alone, others felt that while difficult to build a picture of the informal sector it was possible to analyse changes and assess its training needs through labour market surveys using consistent samples over time. Others pointed to the problems of wage data for the informal sector where the bulk of the people were self-employed. Especially in the rural economy there were a whole range of contractual agreements which would be impossible to capture through wage data. Some suggested that the way out was to collect data on trends in earnings for those who were self-employed.

While not separately discussed there was general agreement that a manpower planning unit, either located in the Planning or Labour Ministry, could make a useful and important contribution to the better development and utilization of human resources. Its work should, however, be mainly concentrated on analysing trends and changes in the labour market rather than carrying out mechanistic manpower projections. There was a need for well-trained economists to be working in such units (preferably, according to *George Psacharopoulos*, Ph.D.s from Anglo-Saxon universities!). Psacharopoulos's idea, however, that the ILO should develop a cookbook on the do's and don'ts for the manpower planning unit was not seriously pursued although it led to a lively discussion with *Samuel Cohen* arguing that such cookbooks could not only be misleading but also strongly present the case of the pro-market ideologues. *Eddy Lee* put this discussion and fears at rest by stating that while the ILO could certainly convey to its field structure the major conclusions of this workshop it was not presumptuous enough to attempt producing a cookbook. *Eddy Lee* pointed out that what had clearly emerged was the need for labour market monitoring and analysis and that the findings of the workshop would be reflected in the design and shift in emphasis in the ILO's analytical and research work.

Index